CONTEMPORARY DECORATING

Front cover photographs: (top left) Robert Harding Syndication/Homes & Gardens/Pia Tryde;
(top right) L. G. Harris (tel: +44 1527 575 441); (bottom left) Robert Harding Syndication/Options/Nick Pope;
(bottom right) Robert Harding Syndication/Homes & Gardens.
Back cover: Abode Interiors.

Photographs page 1: Elizabeth Whiting and Associates/Mark Nicholson; page 3: Ariadne, Holland;
page 4: Ambiance range from Harlequin Fabrics and Wallcoverings (tel: +44 1509 813112);
pages 5-6: Eaglemoss/Graham Rae.

First published in North America
in 1998 by Betterway Books
an imprint of F&W Publications, Inc.
1507 Dana Avenue
Cincinnati, Ohio 45207
1-800-289-0963

ISBN 1-55870-505-8

Printed in Hong Kong

10 9 8 7 6 5 4 3 2 1

CONTEMPORARY DECORATING

BETTERWAY BOOKS
Cincinnati, Ohio

CONTENTS

CREATING THE LOOK

PLAYFUL COLORS AND PATTERNS

DO-IT-YOURSELF DECORATIVE EFFECTS

INDEX

INTRODUCING CONTEMPORARY STYLE

*One of the most rewarding aspects of home design is
choosing a room style – creating a look to suit you,
your home and lifestyle.*

The modern home combines many functions: it is a place of work, rest and play and ideally it should combine beauty with comfort and practicality. A home must also reflect your tastes and those of your family – the secret of good design is reconciling all these sometimes conflicting requirements.

The first problem is finding the right style for the particular room. Start by looking at what you've got. Consider the function of the room, then look at its shape, architectural features and the quality of the light.

In some cases these will suggest a definite direction. This book will help you filter and prioritize your ideas. The first section "Creating the Look" reviews the range of contemporary styles, identifying and analysing the key components so that you can apply them in your own home.

Other rooms may be less interesting initially but even box-like rooms have a surprising amount of scope for a wide range of style options.

Colour and pattern can radically change the appearance and mood of a room. In "Playful Colours and Patterns" the characteristics and impact of the modern palette are considered. You will learn about the way families of colours work, and find schemes and themes to inspire you.

Modern paints and materials are so easy to use that even the novice can achieve creative and effective results. In "Do-It-Yourself Decorative Effects" you will find exciting and easy to follow step-by-step paint effects and projects with which you can transform your home.

The simplicity of these pressed-leaf pictures is typical of contemporary style. Pared-down details and natural materials are strong style pointers.

Here, warm, pale neutrals create a sense of space. Furniture in soft, natural textures enhances this feeling, and the effect is enlivened with style details in a subtle blend of glowing spice tones.

CONTEMPORARY STYLE

Modern, period or unusual conversion homes are all good starting points for airy and uncluttered contemporary style, and you can adapt this essentially young and fashionable style to fit most budgets and circumstances.

Throughout the variations of the style, the constants to aim for are simple and streamlined; creating a feeling of light and space is paramount, whether you choose palest neutrals or brilliant colours as part of your theme.

For a trendsetting decorator look which reflects up-to-the-moment colour and furnishing trends, you may opt for the bold and modish apartment style, and furnish with smart, pared-down or hi-tech basics and colour statement furnishings. For a more adaptable feel, appropriate to informal family living, you can create the more muted look of the soft modern contemporary style by drawing on traditional and contemporary sources for inspiration. Here you could use light, fresh colours for walls and furniture, combined with brighter accents for soft furnishings to create a pleasing, welcoming look.

Whichever direction you choose, aim for simplicity. Keep in mind functional storage, clean-lined furniture and unfussy details as these are all important in creating the contemporary look.

This contemporary bedroom combines comfort with simple details and colour – echoed in the leaf motifs, topiaries, pale wood and fibre flooring.

CONTEMPORARY GRAPHICS

Comic book graphics, cartoon imagery and many contemporary art styles have had a refreshing, creative influence on modern textiles and wallcoverings. A lighthearted approach to surface pattern and a quick-change philosophy, one where prints can be regarded as seasonal or just for fun, means the big bold print you like – but are not sure for how long – can be a design option. You can make a splashy feature with a signature design, using it for a simple pair of curtains, window blind or cushions, or for other relatively inexpensive furnishings. You can then change them when the mood takes you.

Favourite styles include the sketchy look, with darkly outlined shapes filled in with paintbox colours, or softer crayon lines or watercolour effects. Most have a spontaneous look, and are full of vitality.

The culinary details illustrated on these pretty pink curtains have all the spontaneity of a watercolour sketch. The freely drawn style contrasts well with the controlled, colour-matched stripes and checks used elsewhere.

This bright and modern study of contemporary tableware is tailor-made for a kitchen or informal dining area. In different scale coordinates, the effect is light and bright and full of fun.

CONTEMPORARY FLORALS

Soft, modern-style florals are unfussy, with clear colours and graphic qualities – in keeping with the style. Found as medium- to large-scale designs, these florals make a simple statement, contributing to a light and airy feel with their pale backgrounds. Use these florals for informal curtain treatments with toning plains and neutrals; with stripes and checks for upholstery; and with low-key coordinating ranges as part of a soft, total look.

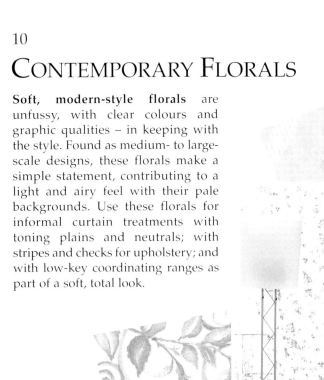

Apartment-style florals create a large-scale, lively splash. Often portrayed as vibrant, stylized brush-stroke flowers, colour is the key to these florals. In a room style that relies on streamlined, minimalist looks, florals work hard here to justify their appearance. Often with a white or brightly coloured background, they glow as pastel brights, hot citrus colours and strong contrasts. They look their best as bedlinen, or as a stunning window blind, and as a focal point sofa or chair cover, teamed with contrast or toning plains.

Soft Modern Hall

*Whether your home is in a modern building or a period property,
you can tailor the soft modern style to suit your hall. Use its agreeable,
adaptable looks to present a smart yet relaxed front to the world.*

On entering a soft modern hall, one of the first impressions is of light and colour – not in an obtrusive way, but as part of a pleasing and uncluttered setting for everyday comings-and-goings. Period details sit happily alongside more avant-garde, modern items. Furnishings and accessories may also hint at ethnic or rustic country influences – both in colour and design – but without overstating their presence. The ease with which these sometimes quite different elements blend together is a definitive characteristic of this relaxed contemporary look.

A noticeable aspect of the soft modern hall is the way flair and function work together, ensuring that practical considerations such as storage also look attractive. Coat hooks, shoe cupboards, telephone tables and doormats are all chosen for their stylish, low-key looks as well as for their usefulness, and pictures, flower or plant displays for their welcoming, stylish impact.

A glowing chilli red colour scheme complements the simplicity of this hallway, with its sensible storage solutions and easy-care surfaces. This approach is typical of the soft modern style, where comfort and practicality are a basic premise, and clean-lined accessories provide attractive finishing touches.

CREATING THE STYLE

The soft modern decorating approach suits any hall shape, with its aim for an overall effect that is unfussy and as spacious looking as possible.

On the walls, plain or broken colour effects in pale, warm tones or rich but muted shades all help to create a genial atmosphere. Harmonious colours – close partners on the colour wheel – or gentle contrast colour schemes, are more appropriate than stronger complementaries or bold patterns.

If the hall has a picture or chair rail, you can create a cosy effect with a darker colour below the rail and a lighter one above and on the ceiling. Alternatively, maximize a feeling of space with the same colour above and below the rail. You can emphasize the hall shape by highlighting the wood-work – door frames, skirtings and picture rails – with a contrast colour, or minimize the busy effect of too many doors or odd angles with walls and woodwork in the same colour, or closely toning shades.

Define the floor shape with durable and streamlined floor covering such as blonde or mid-tone woodstrip flooring, stripped and polished boards, or neutral fitted carpet. Alternatively, customize the floor shape with linoleum – in a traditional inlay pattern, or with classic chequered tiles.

STYLE POINTERS

 WALLS Pale/plain: neutrals; self-colour textures; subtle stripes, checks, colourwash paint effects; muted warm colours; contrast trimwork.

 WINDOWS Curtains/blinds: informal variations of classic curtain styles; relaxed swags and drapes; soft pelmets; wood or metal poles; wooden-slatted blinds; pleated London blinds.

 FABRICS Naturals/unfussy: plains; cotton voile; stripes; checks; subtle ethnic prints and weaves; stylized florals.

 FLOORING Durable/streamlined: blonde woodstrip; polished boards; fitted sisal, coir matting; neutral twist carpet; inlayed linoleum; period-style tiles; plain, ethnic pattern or striped wool/cotton rugs.

 FURNITURE Light wood/metal: streamlined storage bench and coat stand; period-style hallstand; period/modern chest of drawers; upholstered/wicker chair; radiator covers; clean-lined metal with glass.

 LIGHTING Modern classic/streamlined: updated period styles; glass or colour-matched uplighters; colour accent/neutral tablelamps.

 ACCESSORIES Informal/practical: wood/metal umbrella stand; pale wood picture frames; modern prints/classical engravings; contemporary/simple period-style feature mirror; ironwork/plain ceramic lampbase, simple lampshades; colour accent cushions/vases.

▲ *Busy lifestyles may call for a practical approach to decorating the hall. Here, in soft modern style, the simple, functional layout, with its streamlined wooden flooring, is softened by cheery yellow walls and muted green woodwork.*

▶ *This light-enhancing scheme takes its colour cue from the outstanding design of the traditional floor tiles.* **Streamlined modern furniture** *and accessories are understated and well balanced in their period-style setting.* **Colour-coordinated details** *are plain, simple and elegant, to complement the large expanse of concentrated pattern.* **Metallic accessories** *add gleaming highlights, and carry the eye round the hall.*

HALL FURNISHINGS

Accommodating all the usual hall fittings, furnishings and outdoor clothing can be a challenge, unless the hall space – however small – is well organized. With the relaxed look of the soft modern hall, an understairs space can become a small study area or, with neatly stacked shelving and cupboard storage, a centre for children's toys. As a conventional household store cupboard it will be well lit and tidy, with an attractive, space-saving stacking basket or drawer system.

Light-coloured or painted furniture in beech and pine to match the colour scheme is appropriate. Hall pieces may include a coat rail and a shoe storage settle or cupboard. Other useful additions are a roomy chest of drawers or table with a deep top shelf – useful for the telephone, a tablelamp or flower vase. Iron and wicker designs complement the style – look for metal details such as coat hooks, lampbases and curtain poles, a wicker armchair and storage baskets.

Fabrics in a hallway are usually limited to door and window curtains or simple blinds. Low-key plain voile, linen, calico or subtle stripes, checks and quiet patterns suit the soft modern style. Informal tied, tab or casement headings and gathered curtain styles with soft pelmets are all appropriate. Link up colours through the stair carpet, an area rug or runner, and with cushions, or details in pictures and accessories.

▼ The architectural details and generous proportions of a period-style hall are flattered by the simplicity of soft modern style. Here, the dark carpeted stairs become a focal point against the soft earthy tones and warm whites of the colour scheme.

▲ The centrally placed front door and the generous proportions of the period hallway create the ideal setting for focal point decorations such as these intricate, but low-key, stencilled fruit trees. The streamlined layout and the restricted colour scheme control any risk of fussiness.

In a small hall, or one with a very pale colour scheme, a practical but light aluminium umbrella stand can be more flattering than a traditional design.

Looking smart as an elegant console table, with a curvy metal frame and a glass top, wicker takes on a stylish new look. Far removed from its familiar origins, the rustic texture provides a welcome contrast to the mainly smooth and linear shapes in the hall.

Warm-toned neutrals create a spacious effect in this soft modern hall, with its neat home office under the stairs. The dark painted front door and the curvy iron candelabra create a good tonal balance in a pale scheme.

STYLE DETAILS

A neutral colour scheme, or one based on soft harmonies will need a subtle injection of accent colour for accessories and details to bring it to life and prevent it looking dull. In the soft modern hall the most obvious place for an injection of colour – and texture interest – is in a focal point picture or group of pictures, details in a patterned rug, an occasional cushion, and in tabletop pieces such as a lamp, vase or platter. Metallic accents also suit the style, as does the graphic quality of curvy iron-framed wicker furniture, a decorative iron mirror frame or umbrella stand. Curves and soft shapes also help to balance the straight lines and angles associated with a hallway with its typical stairs, doors, and often long and narrow proportions.

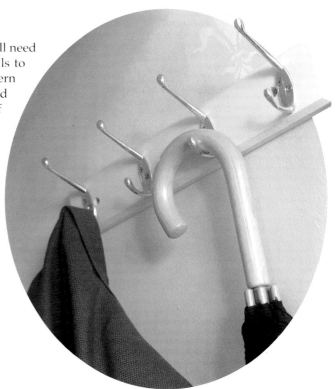

Typical of the style, a practical coat hook fitting with traditional brass hooks blends unobtrusively with the warm, neutral paintwork.

Simple shapes and elegant lines are important factors when choosing soft modern hall accessories. Here, the coolness of the fashionable brushed metal mirror frame and containers is balanced by softer colour elements and highlighted by the vibrant splash of colour in the flowers.

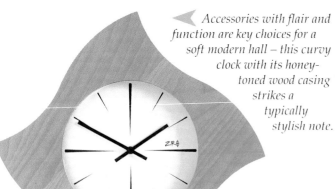

Accessories with flair and function are key choices for a soft modern hall – this curvy clock with its honey-toned wood casing strikes a typically stylish note.

A soft neutral colour scheme and simple, modern styling ensures this understairs "office" area is in keeping with the rest of the decor in the hall, and so much more than just a functional workspace.

SOFT MODERN STUDY

*Whether you work from home, or simply need a handy corner
for paperwork or hobbies, the soft modern study provides versatile
solutions to creating a practical work space.*

In many modern households, finding a space to call
your own – whether you need a home office, a
capsule study or somewhere to pursue a pastime –
can require some imaginative thinking. With limited
space available, compromise is usually necessary, and
so creating a study as part of a dual-purpose area is
often the most practical solution.

Luckily, the soft modern style has the kind of relaxed
looks, furniture and furnishings that are easily adapted
– functional features do not have to look overtly so, nor
do they need to be heavily disguised to blend with the
existing scheme. The style is sufficiently flexible for
you to fit shelving and work storage into an alcove or

▲ *Often sharing space in a living room area, the soft modern
study relies on neat, functional storage, clean lines and soft
colours to promote a sense of order and efficiency. Office storage
and desktop accessories (inset) are both practical and attractive.*

corner in a living room, hallway or landing, or even site
a desk unit close to a bed without spoiling the effect of
the main decor. A soft colour scheme with low-key
patterns, fluid styling, warm wood colours and neat,
functional furniture are the starting points, while
bright ideas for display and storage solutions can turn
any space into an attractive, tailor-made study.

CREATING THE STYLE

The most spacious option for locating a study is often a guest bedroom or loft conversion, but it is possible to create a well-planned area to accommodate your needs elsewhere. The most important considerations are an uncluttered worktop, good seating, effective lighting and well-planned, neat storage. If you work with a computer, your primary needs are probably quite simple: a well-positioned work station – preferably with separate shelves for monitor, keyboard and printer – a comfortable chair, good natural and desktop lighting, adequate filing and reference storage and a noticeboard. These modest needs can often be met in capsule form – if not actually in a cupboard, perhaps in a space not unlike one.

A small-scale study is obviously the easiest to accommodate in any size home. Choose a worktop material to blend with other furniture in a living room or bedroom, while storage cupboards can coordinate with the styles of existing pieces or units. Fit wardrobe-style cupboards with shelves and wire stacking baskets, and put dividers in drawers. In the soft modern study, standard office-type furniture such as metal filing cabinets are not always ideal; one option is to screen off the working corner with a folding panel screen, covered with fabric to match soft furnishings, or aim to blend filing cabinets into the decor – perhaps as desktop supports under a pale wood worktop. If the study is sited in an alcove, you can fit folding doors, or simply hang a roller blind to cover the area if you want it to be out of sight when it is not in use.

For a workroom-study where you need space to spread out materials – for dressmaking, craft or artwork, for example – a large worktop and clear floor space are the ideal. In a limited or multi-use space, a removable work surface is essential; trestles can look functional and stylish, and a foldaway worktop is practical. Both can be cleared into a cupboard or stored under a bed.

STYLE POINTERS

 WALLS Plain/subtle: pale or energizing yet muted matt latex; sponging or colourwashing; low-key wallcoverings; stripes or texture; wood panelling to chair rail height.

 WINDOWS Curtains/blinds: simple, informal curtain styles; relaxed, soft pelmets; iron or wood curtain poles; wood-slat Venetian, Roman or London blinds.

 FLOORING Neutral/plain: woodstrip flooring with rugs; natural fibre matting; fitted plain carpet.

 FABRICS Unfussy: cotton plains, stripes or checks for curtains and upholstery; also relaxed, low-key florals for curtains/blinds; fitted covers for divan.

 FURNITURE Streamlined/compact: pale wood, colourwashed, limed or dragged, light-colour paint-effect wood for desk, shelves, chests of drawers; plain colour sofabed; tailored divan cover.
Shelving: glass and brushed/white metal supports; wood with decorative shelf trims.
Seating: comfortable and practical desk chair, or domestic chair at good desk/table height; slipcover for upright chair.

 LIGHTING: Direct/diffused: a directional desklamp; wall lights/uplighters; table lamps; soft pendant light; dimmer switches.

 ACCESSORIES Functional/decorative: fabric-covered noticeboard; wicker/steamed wood/fabric-covered wastebasket; coordinating colour/fabric file boxes; clean-lined graphics clock; pale wood/clear glass picture frames; high-tech plastic/fabric hanging files.

➤ *A low-key colour scheme, based on warm neutrals and subtle pattern interest, creates a relaxed setting in a dual-purpose room.*
Simple, streamlined furniture lends itself well to both the working study and bedroom areas of the room.
The purpose-designed desk unit and chair are practical and well sited under the uncluttered window.
Curtain dividers effectively screen the bed when required and soften the general effect.

An alcove can offer all the space you require for a capsule study. A purpose-designed computer table holds essential equipment at a good working height, and fitted shelving ensures that neatly coordinating folders and files are within easy reach.

STUDY FURNISHINGS

The soft modern study is an unassuming area – almost a chameleon in its adaptability. As it blends with the character of whatever room it inevitably shares with – living room, bedroom or spare room – as well as fitting in with the general decor in a more open area such as a hallway or landing, low-key looks are essential. Soft furnishings and furniture style will take their colour and pattern lead from the main decor.

As with all soft modern furnishings, the emphasis is on relaxed, easy styling, using natural fabrics such as cotton and linen for window treatments and upholstery. If the study is in a spare bedroom, a tailored, box-pleated cover will look neat on a divan and make it less bed-like, or consider investing in a sofabed or futon. Choose low-key or neutral colours to blend quietly with the scheme. A window blind may be practical in the study area, but any accompanying curtain treatment to soften the effect should follow the style of curtains on adjacent windows.

You can transform a functional pinboard by covering it with fabric to blend with the scheme – a toning plain, print, stripe or check. If wall space is a problem, attach the notice-board to the inside of a cupboard door, or create an alternative display area on one side of a folding fabric-covered screen.

For a spacious look, match the study flooring with the rest of the room, or try to blend it with the adjacent area. It may be practical to place a rug under the desk and chair, so choose a design or plain colour to complement the other furnishings.

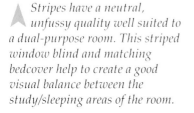

Stripes have a neutral, unfussy quality well suited to a dual-purpose room. This striped window blind and matching bedcover help to create a good visual balance between the study/sleeping areas of the room.

As an inventive solution to accommodating a home study in a bedroom, this closet office earns a style prize: the look is elegant and restrained, as well as neat and practical.

On a lighthearted note, furniture and accessories in this study area are decorated with postage stamps. Following a decorative theme in this way also helps to "pull" a look together, especially where you are combining unmatched pieces in your study.

Keeping clutter under control is a feature of soft modern style. In this versatile study/bedroom unit, basket shelves add visual interest with their change of texture.

An understairs area is often surprisingly roomy, with potential for a study area. Here, a long worktop and attractively detailed units offer space for a practical study area without compromising the character of the hall.

STYLE DETAILS

Desktop accessories and stationery can look dull, but it is possible to find attractive, home office items with a bit of colour and design flair. Shiny metal index containers; attractive pigeon-hole chests which you can paint, and stylish cardboard and clear plastic hanging and desk storage units are available from some art and design shops and graphics suppliers. You can also cover box files and folders with fabric or paper to tone with a scheme. Softening the effect, without compromising the basic, practical requirements of office accessories, makes an integrated home study more user friendly.

If you barely have room to squeeze in a work station, this hanging shelf could be an imaginative compromise. The shelf has a conventional back support and strong rope ties to keep the surface steady.

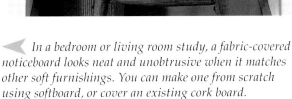

In a bedroom or living room study, a fabric-covered noticeboard looks neat and unobtrusive when it matches other soft furnishings. You can make one from scratch using softboard, or cover an existing cork board.

File boxes and notebooks need not be boring or dull. These designs are typical of many simple and stylish stationery items that look good in their own right.

The humble wastebin is an essential in the home study. Choose a design to complement your colour scheme – this one would look good in a low-key neutral setting.

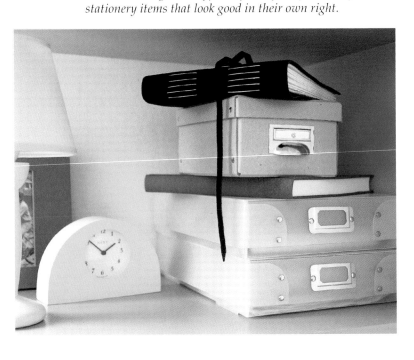

SOFT MODERN BEDROOM

*The relaxed, mainstream style of the contemporary soft modern
bedroom draws inspiration from the streamlined looks of contemporary
design and the comfortable qualities of traditional materials.*

In today's homes, practical considerations
for decorations and furnishings are
as essential an element as looks
and style – so a bedroom designed
to integrate these elements is an
attractive option. The contemporary
soft modern bedroom achieves
this practical stylishness with
a casual informality that belies
a disciplined approach to
clutter. The overall look is
fresh – blending the clean lines
of contemporary design with more
traditional features – and the
atmosphere is calm and relaxing.
Soft, muted colours and a balance
of contrasting textures; rough and

*In a typically low-key scheme, soft yellow and
warm neutrals balance the golden pine tones of
a traditional wooden sleigh bed. Metallic
accents for accessories – seen in the picture
frames and curtain print, and in the quirky,
contemporary mirror frame (left), add sparks
of colour to an otherwise subtle room.*

smooth, shiny and matt, combine in
light-enhancing schemes, with pale
and honeyed wood tones, natural
materials and discreet metallic accents.
Space-saving storage solutions such as
underbed drawers or boxes, stacking or
hanging shelves and sensible shoe racks
all help to create a calm, comfortable
atmosphere that's thoroughly modern in style.

CREATING THE STYLE

As the success of the soft modern bedroom owes much to its uncluttered looks, choose a pale or mid-tone colour scheme with no strong colour contrasts. This will help to create a restful, spacious look – you can create a pool of pattern or colour with the bedlinen, and possibly, coordinated curtains. Neutral and natural colours and fabrics come into their own in the soft modern setting, as do gentle harmonies and contrasts, with metallic or colour accents for interest. A few well-chosen accents, such as tiebacks and cushion covers, can save coordinates from any risk of blandness or uniformity, and give the scheme a personal touch.

Capitalize on architectural features such as coving and mouldings, by treating them as subtle "visual breaks" – you can use softly toning colours above and below a chair or picture rail, or create a similar effect with simple stencilled borders.

Pale-coloured flooring helps create a spacious feel – blonde woodstrip, light tiles or a neutral carpet are ideal. Bleached and colourwashed boards are another option, teamed with soft-toned rugs.

STYLE POINTERS

 WALLS Pale/subtle: neutrals and mid-tone latex; soft paint effects such as colourwashing/sponging.
Wallcoverings: self-coloured pattern motifs; subtle stripes, coordinating borders and trims.

 WINDOWS Curtains/blinds: informal variations of formal styles; full length with gathered or tab headings; soft pelmets and swags; metal/light wood curtain poles; matching tiebacks, metal holdbacks.
Blinds: softly structured, Austrian, Roman, London blind; shaped-edge roller blind; wooden Venetians.

 FABRICS Unfussy/naturals: neutral cottons, checks, stripes, soft, stylized florals, coordinate prints; plain and printed voiles; muslin; plain colour cotton/silk accents.
Bedlinen: pale, cotton plains, self-coloured stripes, jacquards; fresh, coordinate prints; button/tie fastenings; Oxford-style pillowcases; gathered valances.

 FLOORING Neutral/plain: pale woodstrip/block styles; stripped boards; plain fitted carpet/sisal/coir matting; linoleum, tiles.
Rugs: kelim/ethnic motif; cream or neutral wool; striped cotton mats.

 FURNITURE Streamlined/informal: modern or traditional shapes in blonde and mid-tone woods – beech, pine, colourwashed/limed wood; built-in or freestanding wardrobes; metal-framed pieces with cane/wicker; slip-covered chair; ottoman/blanket box.
Bed: simple lines, period-style brass, traditional sleigh bed; metal or slatted pine bedstead; Shaker-style or cane headboards; underbed box storage.

 LIGHTING Diffused/simple: low-key, cone pendant; streamlined iron chandelier; wall uplighters/sconces; candlestick/plain ceramic table lampbases, parchment/natural shades; expanding/angle arm, metal/coloured reading lights; dimmer switches.

 ACCESSORIES Informal/modern: casual throws; buttoned envelope cushions; coloured/clear glass or pottery vases; simple flower arrangements; light wood picture frames/box frames; botanical studies/art prints/photos; wicker baskets; ironwork candlesticks.

A striking coordinate print for bedlinen and matching curtains is complemented by soothing plains and pale neutrals. Balancing patterns in this way is typical of the soft modern approach, where bold prints are used with discretion.

▶ *A soft colour scheme creates a restful soft modern atmosphere and a feeling of space. The casually draped curtain, with its contrast edgings and bow tieback is elegant yet informal. Honey coloured pine furniture and a roomy wicker chair blend easily into their pale setting. Simply-styled bedlinen and soft furnishings in natural cotton fabrics are a typical choice for a soft modern room. The metal wall sconce creates a subtle contrast with the light background and honey-coloured wood furniture. Colourwashed picture frames, black and white prints and a botanical study are attractive, understated accessories.*

BEDROOM FURNISHINGS

To create the fresh look associated with contemporary soft modern style, balance plain and patterned elements carefully. Typical choices for bedlinen or curtains are fresh stripes, checks and stylized florals on clear, pale or white backgrounds, teamed with toning plains or coordinates.

Almost any kind of bed – from a plain divan to a traditional brass bed works with soft modern style, as the type of bedlinen you select really underlines the look. Layer crisp cotton sheets with a simple duvet, followed by a folded throw or blanket, and top these with standard and continental square pillows. Choose bedlinen with contemporary detailing such as ties, piping, contrast borders or button fastenings. Cotton percale and cotton mixes, satin-cotton designs and heavier, damask weaves all work well.

Complement the bed with a low-key curtain treatment – styles which have tab headings on a curly iron or wooden pole, or softly gathered styles with a simple fabric or painted pelmet, or with unfussy roll-up or wooden-slatted Venetian blinds.

Freestanding wardrobes can match a bed or dressing table, or can be built in to maximize space. Either style may be painted or colourwashed to blend with the walls – adding to a spacious effect – or have streamlined, pale wood doors which pull back to reveal an impressive and compact storage layout. If space in the room is really tight, replace the doors of a built-in wall unit with simple roll-up blinds, choosing a colour to blend with the scheme.

Create a soothing atmosphere with low-key, but effective lighting. A central fitting – which can range from a sleek, iron chandelier to a simple cone shape or glass fitting – benefits from a dimmer switch. Bedside and table lamps can vary from pared-down modern styles in plastic, wood and glass or metal, to simple candle-stick shapes fitted with paper shades.

▲ *Low-key and serene, vanilla white and soft green create a restful theme. The effect owes much to the symmetry of the scheme, where straight lines and soft textures are echoed through the fabrics and wicker table.*

▶ *Pine furniture has a chameleon's ability to blend into many different room styles. In a soft modern setting, crisp bedlinen, red accents and uncluttered styling are carefully balanced to complement the warm wood tones.*

◀ Tartan checks in citrus harmonies add a colour splash against a pastel lemon background, while coordinated pottery adds low-key accents. Pale, colourwashed pine furniture and the bleached wood floor balance the patterns and help to create a spacious atmosphere.

▶ One of the assets of the soft modern bedroom is the option to blend period features and modern styles together to create a fresh new look. Here, the iron bed and white cotton coverlet echo the past, while the soft furnishings and neatly chequered floor have a contemporary feel.

▼ The calming neutrals in this scheme are balanced through a blend of pale wood tones and soft, natural textures, as seen in the woven bedhead, cotton bedlinen and fleece rug. A spark of colour in the patterned bed throw and a metallic gleam in the reading light and gold sculpture all add lively accents.

BEDROOM DETAILS

As with all soft modern furnishings, details are understated and unfussy. Aim to keep clutter at bay – neaten the dressing table or the tops of chests – by storing toiletries and accessories in containers or drawers whenever possible. Organize their contents with drawer dividers, or keep bits and pieces tidy in neatly stacked fabric-covered boxes or in wicker baskets.

A few elegant flowers arranged in a curvy modern glass vase will complement straight lines and mainly plain backgrounds, as will a themed collection of graphic prints in clean-lined picture frames. As for mirrors, choose frames in simple, contemporary shapes, with metal, pale wood or colourwashed finishes. Box frames and frames with multiple openings look sleek and smart arranged in rows or small groups – above the bed or over a chest of drawers.

Incorporate as many practical space-saving features as you can into the bedroom. Simple calico hanging shelves and shoe tidies, as well as underbed storage boxes all help to maintain the ordered look that is typical of the style.

Clever storage is the key to the soft modern look. Introduce shelves, drawers and baskets to maximise wardrobe space; utilize alcoves or built-in wardrobe space in this way. Hide everything behind pale wood-panelled doors or doors painted to blend with the scheme.

This citrus-fresh colour scheme is complemented with lashings of white, and bedlinen in a simple, contemporary design. The daisy print on a background of checks has a fashionably retro-look which is entirely in keeping with easy-going soft modern style.

Pale, colourwashed picture frames suit the soft modern style, where their understated looks flatter furnishings and other details. Here, pictures are grouped above the bed, complementing the fresh blue and white bedlinen.

APARTMENT LIVING ROOM

Make the most of your precious free time with a flexible living space that allows you to relax in style. An apartment living room is sleekly, boldly bright, and strong on innovative design.

Meet the challenge of modern living head-on with an upbeat room to relax and unwind in. Plain, confidently coloured walls, furniture with simple, clean lines and high-tech materials such as steel and glass sit happily side by side in the apartment style living room. Add sensuously satisfying textures – a warm furry throw or plush velvet cushions – for a sense of comfort and luxury. Cool, bare wood floors are softened by deep pile rugs; light floods in through windows uncluttered by heavy curtains and blinds.

Many contemporary style items of furniture make a design feature of flexibility: coffee tables move on giant castors, occasional tables double as trays. An apartment living room has a clean, calm look; bare, plain surfaces are more restful to the eye and easier to clean. A single flower in a quirky vase, or a pale wooden bowl piled with vivid green apples, makes a strong statement. Unusual colour combinations catch the mood – deep slate-purple with lime green, pale turquoise and chestnut brown, fuchsia and lemon yellow – forget your inhibitions and have fun.

Brilliant paintbox colours and simple boxy shapes give a fresh, young appeal to an apartment style living room. Tubular steel tables and lamps combine with modern prints and stylish accessories, such as the candlesticks (right), for an unmistakably contemporary style look.

CREATING THE STYLE

The look is based on pared-down simplicity, with plain surfaces that focus on colour and texture rather than pattern. Period details don't fit in with apartment style – paint them in with the surrounding surface so they disappear. If you have a fireplace, play it down by painting it to match the walls or replace it with a very simple, chunky wood or stone surround. Walls are painted to create flat planes of colour which emphasize the shape of the room. Neutral tones are restful, and sometimes have a faintly metallic, burnished effect. Or choose clear primary or secondary hues – chrome yellow, rich purple, acid green or turquoise. Pastels work well too – mauves and lilacs are particularly cool and fresh.

Try painting the walls in different colours – for example, one wall in a strong yellow, and the others in varying shades of grey; accentuate any asymmetrical features, perhaps a sloping ceiling or a big pillar, with colour.

If you prefer wallpaper, choose plain, paint effect designs rather than patterns. Leave paintwork white or take it one tone darker or lighter than the walls, and choose a matt finish. Plain, flush doors are in keeping; change door furniture to sleek aluminium in modern shapes.

Apartment style floors are hard – wood strip, parquet or stripped and sanded boards, all finished if possible in a light tone. Hardwearing rubber flooring is also popular. If you want a softer feel, choose a plain, short-pile fitted carpet in steel grey or beige. Designer rugs in bold, painterly designs or geometric shapes are also an important feature.

STYLE POINTERS

 WALLS Plain/bold: matt latex in strong, clear colours; sophisticated neutrals or pale pastels in quirky mixes.
Wallpapers: subtle metallic sheen, or surface effects such as rough plaster or limewash in strong colours.

 WINDOWS Curtains: simple panels of unlined fabric, eyeletted or clipped on tension wire or steel pole.
Blinds: Roman, roller, wooden-slatted or metal Venetian, pleated styles.

 FLOORS Hard: wooden floor in light shades; plain fitted carpet; industrial-type rubber or vinyl tiles.
Rugs: abstract or geometric designs in strong colours; imitation animal skin; sixties' style fluffy rugs.

 FABRICS Contemporary: prints and weaves in bold abstract or geometric designs; plain cotton, linen in neutrals or strong colours; velvet, silk in brilliant colours; modern textural weaves using Lycra and metallic threads.

 FURNITURE Streamlined: curvy or square-cut sofas with simple lines; plain upholstery and wooden or metal legs; high-tech leather and steel chairs; modular stacking units, industrial steel shelving, glass shelves on steel supports.

 LIGHTING Futuristic: tiny spots in ceiling or on wire tracking systems; anglepoise lamp; floor uplighters; table lamps in steel, glass, wood and parchment.

 ACCESSORIES Sparse/stylish: simple designer ceramics, glass and coloured plastics; prints of modern art in simple frames; potted cacti or large architectural plants; strongly coloured and boldly shaped flowers in simple bunches or singly.

◀ In this apartment style living room, cool blues in a plain, matt finish provide an uncluttered background for the simple lines of the furniture and window blinds. Against the neutral furnishings, fuchsia pink – in the framed print and flower display – creates dynamic colour contrast.

▲ **Subtly textured and coloured walls** offer a cool backdrop for a collection of sketches and the distinctive shapes of lamps and seating.
A simply styled asymmetric sofa is covered in an unusual shade of purple, perfect for an apartment style room.
Functional steel shelving provides storage and display space.
An anglepoise lamp and neon wall fitting provide flexible contemporary style task or atmospheric lighting.

APARTMENT STYLE FURNISHINGS

Simple shapes with clean lines in clear, strong colours characterize apartment style furniture. The look is relaxed and practical, but strong on good design. Bold colours are tempered by natural textures: wood is pale and lightly waxed; steel or aluminium details are important.

Sofas are either chunky and square, or have elegantly curving backs and arms, often asymmetric, and smoothly upholstered rather than plumply cushioned. Tapering wooden or metal legs add to the streamlined look. Coverings are generally plain, strong colours or neutrals – you can add cushions for contrast and interest.

Look for contemporary classic sling chairs in leather and steel, or choose curvy sixties' style in preformed plastic – you may find something second hand.

Coffee tables are pale wood or steel and glass, some with giant castors or wheels; others have useful shelves underneath, or act as display cabinets for your stylish accessories.

▶ *A distinctive designer rug can act as the focus for the whole room. Pick out accent colours, such as the burnt orange and turquoise in this rug, for splashes of colour in accessories round the room, set against a calming neutral background.*

▲ *Light flooding in at the bare, uncluttered windows picks out bright, bold colours and unusual shapes in this contemporary living room. Lime green velvet and spiralling steel feet give the curvy sofa film star glamour; the pale floorboards are warmed by a kaleidoscopic rug in hot reds, pinks and yellows.*

A streamlined sofa is a key feature in an apartment style living room. In bright berry red, this one demonstrates the desired effect, as it contrasts with the table colours and the hot mustard walls.

Colouring walls in this way accentuates the shape of the space you live in as well as the objects contained in it. The flowing curves of the daybed set up yet another interesting contrast against the stark straight lines of the walls and ceiling.

Opt for simply styled, modular storage for books, music systems and TV equipment. Black stained ash effect looks snappy, or choose a pale, lightly varnished wood. Alternatively, choose industrial-looking steel shelving – try catering or office suppliers – for a more open display.

Lighting makes a strong design statement, and is well planned for atmosphere and convenience. Site low voltage ceiling spots close to walls to highlight pictures and display items, or fit tension wire tracking systems for adjustable lighting. Look for wall lights with space-age styling in steel and aluminium and glass. Floorstanding up or downlighters have bendy steel stems, or smoothly sculptured pale wood posts; or go for spiky black hi-tech halogen lamps that you can angle in any direction. Table lamps may be moulded in fibreglass or have smoothly shaped wooden bases and fifties' style drum lampshades; other designs use eco-friendly parchment twirled in sculptural spirals.

Windows are kept as clear as possible. A single panel of brightly patterned fabric or voile may be hung on a high-tension wire or steel pole; otherwise opt for a simple fabric Roman or roller blind, or choose a Venetian or pleated blind in a neutral or strong colour.

STYLE DETAILS

Choose apartment style accessories with care – splash out on a single designer bowl or huge glass vase rather than lots of small items. A single flower in a slender container can be as effective as a showy mixed bunch; pictures are often casually propped against the wall rather than hung. Details are often witty and amusing – huge industrial-looking wheels and castors, comma-shaped steel or colourful cast resin shapes for handles. Plastic and polythene has come of age in clever and colourful accessories – photo frames, wastepaper baskets, candlesticks and bowls.

▽ *A fresh approach to design results in furniture and lighting full of exciting new shapes, colour combinations and details. A spiral of parchment turns a long fluorescent tube into a sculptural exercise in lighting.*

△ *Coolly minimalist, a row of single lilies in narrow flutes set up a linear rhythm on a mantelpiece. A tiny photograph, carefully framed, makes another compelling detail.*

◁ *The clever design of this contemporary style lamp floods both shade and base with light, so that both colours glow equally strongly. The black bowl of lemons links both with the foot of the lamp and the glowing yellow base.*

▽ *Eliminating colour and pattern concentrates attention on clever shaping and texture – here the steel table legs and the gracefully flaring vase echo the shapes of the tulips.*

APARTMENT KITCHEN

*Streamlined, functional and bright, an apartment-style kitchen
meets the needs of modern living. Clean lines and a minimum of
detail make it economical to create and easy to work in.*

A kitchen that suits your lifestyle is vitally important, and if your pace of life is fast you need a kitchen that is easy to care for, smart to look at and inviting to use. The apartment-style kitchen takes advantage of every "hi-tech" development: industrial-style surfaces, ultra-modern appliances, all the latest designer gadgets, and confident, bold colour schemes. Careful planning and innovative design solutions make the most of every corner,

clearing away clutter to give an impression of airy space and light.

This is an ideal look to go for if you have a limited budget or space is at a premium, as the greatest strength of an apartment-style kitchen is its emphasis on compact, functional design rather than the decorative. Economical white melamine units with stainless steel trim and streamlined easy-clean surfaces are entirely in keeping with the look, as are shiny steel kitchen utensils and appliances.

An unexpected colour scheme of lilac, turquoise and scarlet enhances the imaginative use of space in this kitchen. Tiny touches of black – a doorknob, the clock case, and a curvy pot or two – lend definition and balance to the unusual mix of colours.

CREATING THE LOOK

The keyword for an apartment-style kitchen is practicality. You don't need a lot of space to have an efficient, labour-saving kitchen – even a galley kitchen can be a pleasure to use. An island unit may solve space problems, giving additional work, storage or even eating areas. Look around for unusual, utilitarian materials: for instance, you could replace part of an internal or even external wall with glass bricks. These have a chunky industrial look, and let light through while still obscuring the view. A sliding glass door, or folding door, may help with space; a modern flush panel door is better than the traditional panelled style. Inexpensive materials such as plywood and medium density fibreboard are now quite acceptable, simply waxed or varnished.

For the walls, choose marble or granite-effect tiling or sleek black or white ceramic. Set these finishes against plain, painted walls in pure slabs of flat colour – lots of pristine white, muted neutrals, or sharp citrus tones for a crisp and stylish effect. Or you may prefer the more restful, subtle tones of mauve or blue.

On the floor, natural finishes such as sealed wood, quarry tiles or slate are beautiful but can be expensive; tough vinyl or linoleum in simple chequerboard black and white, or marled all over patterns, look equally good. Even concrete – stained, waxed and polished – has the right look, or look for studded rubber industrial flooring.

STYLE POINTERS

WALLS AND CEILING Plain/bright: pale ceilings, painted walls in interesting, even daring colours, or subtle mixes of neutrals and pastels, often two or three used in separate areas.
Tiles: black/white ceramic, grey marble or granite-effect ceramic; blocks of mosaic.

WINDOWS Restrained: no curtains; wood or metal Venetian blinds, roller, Roman or roll-up blinds; shutters.

FABRICS Simple: crisp canvas or cotton in plain neutrals or bright clear colours; stripes, checks or modern splashy prints.

FLOORING Tough/functional: ceramic, slate or quarry tiles, plain or very simple design; vinyl or linoleum; sealed strip wood finish.

FURNITURE Streamlined: sleek fitted units with flush doors and neat handles, finished in melamine, natural wood or glass.
Appliances: hi-tech, built-in oven, stove top and hood, microwave; white, grey or steel finishes.
Table/chairs: fixed breakfast bar or wall-mounted table; slimline steel stools or chairs.

LIGHTING Unobtrusive: low-voltage spots inset in ceiling, hi-tech tracking systems, concealed strip lighting.

ACCESSORIES Modern: polished/satin-finish steel or matt black designer appliances – coffeemaker, kettle, toaster, utensils; unusual designer ceramic bowls and glass.

Subtle tones of mauve and white, set off by simple steel handles, make a sophisticated combination in this elegant kitchen. Everything is neatly on hand, from the built-in microwave to the wall-mounted phone. A single piece of designer pottery adds a distinctive decorative touch.

Sleek white fitted units have a cool, hygienic look and simple elegance.
A peninsular breakfast bar makes the most of the space and adds a useful eating area for casual dining.
Space-age appliances – eye-level oven and separate, stainless steel stove top – are carefully sited for convenience.
Delicate blue-green walls and floor increase the sense of space.
Neatly stacked china on the shelves adds interest without clutter.
Discreet downlighters give a clear wash of light across the kitchen.

KITCHEN FURNISHINGS

The most economical, low-budget kitchen units can form the basis for an apartment-style kitchen. Plain flush melamine doors in white or neutral shades of grey, beige and cream are perfect, and if you are buying a new kitchen, there are lots of brighter shades to choose from in lacquered medium density fibreboard or acrylic finishes.

Revamp old melamine doors by swapping old-fashioned handles for stylish steel or curvy wooden ones, for a new look at very little expense. If you have panelled doors, consider replacing the panels with security glass, which has a grid of wire mesh, or tempered glass. Wood is still a classic favourite, but opt for the paler woods such as birch or ash, in a simple, streamlined design.

Few people can afford real marble, granite or beech work-tops, but there are many impressive imitations in hardwearing laminates or other composite materials; or search out catering suppliers for the steel worktops used in restaurant kitchens. It's important to keep clutter tidily out of sight; well-planned storage is the key, leaving a clean sweep of worktop.

Choose cooking appliances in a hygienic white finish, with tempered glass windows and steel trims, or clad in shiny or satin steel for the ultimate in hi-tech.

If your kitchen is big enough, incorporate a breakfast bar or island unit, with a laminated top on steel supports; a wall-mounted, drop-leaf table saves space. Steel or wooden folding chairs, or stylish bar stools with simple metal legs and uphol-stered seats all add to the look. Keep fabrics to a minimum; wide stripes, or a wild print add a splash of colour and soft-ness in a Roman blind, or tight-covered seats on bar stools in a series of brilliant colours.

Lighting should be practical and unobtrusive – small down-lighters, flexible spot systems and undershelf strip lighting are all suitable for the apartment kitchen look.

Drop-in wire mesh bowls, tough steel-encased drawers and steel shelves and worktop present an uncompromisingly workmanlike image, with more shiny steel accessories to reinforce the message. A witty contrast is supplied by the bright colours of three glass bowls and a wacky penguin.

This carefully structured open-plan kitchen gains valuable light from the stairwell. The cool blue, grey and white scheme is restful and quiet, relying for impact on the strong horizontal and vertical lines provided by the chunky black island worktop, asymmetrically supported on a steel pedestal at one end and a blue cupboard at the other.

A severe black and white colour scheme gives cool, apartment-style good looks to a standard, off-the-peg white melamine kitchen. The black and white theme is continued in the tiles on the splashback and in the white floor tiles. The white sink and marble-effect worktops complete the apartment kitchen look.

Black and white takes a classical twist in this low-budget kitchen, here cleverly accented with a black-painted wall and a Greco-Roman style ceramic and moulding. Simple black and white vinyl tiles and a crisply striped drape continue the theme.

Seriously sleek, this kitchen is designed to impress, with its glossy blue lacquered doors, gleaming black tiles and steel trimmings. The clever cutouts in the tops of doors and drawers remove the need for jutting knobs and handles. White accessories and a sculptural, spiky plant spark up the darker tones of the kitchen.

Vibrant slabs of colour are confidently used here like an abstract painting, to enhance a series of horizontal and vertical planes. Charcoal grey shelves placed against a burnt orange wall, a grid of black ceramic mosaic, and a yellow-painted cupboard form a vertical backdrop for the spread of rich jade worktop, perfectly balanced by a yellow bowl of fruit.

STYLE DETAILS

Function is still the theme when it comes to accessories – resist the temptation to add too many decorative bits and pieces. Catering-style steel pans and utensils catch the light, stacked neatly on shelves or hung on steel grids. Splash out on the latest designer gadgets – a space-age lemon squeezer or conical black coffee pot. A single big swirly glass bowl of fruit, or a row of steel storage jars is decoration enough.

A shiny chrome bottle rack holds designer-style condiments within easy reach of work surfaces. Brightly coloured glass storage jars add a contemporary touch to an apartment-style kitchen.

Stark and business-like, a monochrome scheme with gleaming steel accessories makes the perfect apartment-style kitchen. Here, large white tiles create a clean backdrop for a hanging wine rack, an industrial-style steel stove top and hood and shiny appliances.

Cheerful ceramics and containers add colour in this simple, functional kitchen. The ingenious stacking system allows bottles and containers to be stored above work surfaces to maximize space.

Even waste bins have gone space age: these shiny bins have steel lids and pedals – definitely a designer accessory to keep on show.

APARTMENT BEDROOM

*The upbeat apartment bedroom often doubles as a functional
work space. Streamlined furniture and versatile furnishings make the
most of small rooms, and vibrant colour adds bold accents.*

Flair, function and an air of metropolitan chic underline the apartment bedroom. It is a look to suit busy people who like uncluttered, understated design with a practical edge, and want to be spared a bedroom scheme that will take hours of careful pattern matching.

The style is sufficiently adaptable to suit a small bedroom in a modern home, a "starter" studio apartment, or a larger space in an older property. This versatility is a bonus in an open-plan setting, or where the bedroom also does service as a study, a home gym or a living room.

The colour scheme is light and airy and maximizes a feeling of space. Low-key, contemporary furniture – typically in pale-coloured wood and shiny materials such as glass and metal – blends easily into its setting, leaving you free to add unusual but calming colour accents and textural interest with furnishings. Accessories should be selected for their strong design and bold colouring – an abstract rug or an innovative table lamp, a wacky mirror or curvy glass vase are typical apartment-style touches.

▲ Neutral tones and strong colour accents feature in the apartment bedroom, where simple, stylish looks and practical storage solutions are a priority. Contemporary design details such as this bold blue alarm clock with its modern form are typical additions to the scheme.

QUARTZ

CREATING THE STYLE

Pale, solid-toned painted walls, smooth floors and uncluttered windows with simple curtains or blinds create the smart, pared-down look that epitomizes the style. In this setting, natural white, soft pastels and neutrals for walls and woodwork, ceiling and floor create a feeling of space and light, and provide a "blank canvas" for the subtle tones of wood and metal furniture and carefully controlled bursts of colour.

If a plain paint finish seems too stark for your bedroom, soften the effect by using a broken colour on the walls. A subtle colourwash or a stippled paint effect – or a wallcovering that recreates the look – will add depth and create a muted glow.

Blonde woodstrip or woodblock floors are flattering with their cool looks and interesting perspective lines, while fitted sisal flooring or neutral fitted carpet defines the floor area and adds a welcome textural interest to contrast with smooth or shiny surfaces. Light-coloured linoleum, rubber flooring or tiles are another good, practical option.

Lighting should be discreet and stylish, and easily controlled. A dimmer switch is a perfect apartment-style solution, as you can use it to create different moods in an instant. For the lights themselves, functional, minimal designs in metal, glass and plastic are ideal, and double as bedside lights. Wall uplighters have a sculptural quality, and may be glass or metal, or painted to match the background. A central fitting may be a showpiece example of hi-tech design, or a simple industrial-style model in metal or glass.

STYLE POINTERS

 WALLS Plain/neutral: white, light enhancing walls and ceiling; colour block contrasts; graphic stencil/block print motifs. **Wallcoverings:** subtle colourwash effects; checks or stripes.

 WINDOWS Blinds/simple curtains: wooden Venetians, plantation shutters; pale/white Roman/roller blinds; neutral rod pocket/tab-headed curtain styles on wooden/metal poles; white voile/muslin drapes.

 FABRICS Neutrals/striking colour: natural linen; crisp white cotton/self patterned weaves; slubb silks; checks; stripes; stylized, abstract florals/graphic prints.

 FLOORING Sleek/neutral: woodstrip/polished/painted floorboards; natural fibre matting; plain wool fitted carpet; bold geometric/designer rugs; cotton dhurries.

 FURNITURE Clean-lined/space saving: contemporary look, dual purpose, blonde wood: chests of drawers, dressing table/desk; pale/neutral fitted cupboards/free standing units; forged iron/glass/wicker; moulded plastic units. **Bed:** plain divan with underbed storage; streamlined head and footboard/modern four poster styles; forged iron; futon; sofa bed.

 LIGHTING Elegant/practical: wall mounted uplighters; streamlined office-style task lamps; sculptural/architectural glass, plastic, metallic lampbases/shades; dimmer switches; halogen spotlights/high-tech fittings.

 ACCESSORIES Streamlined/colourful: bold, curvy plain/coloured glass/plastic or brushed steel/dark metallic containers, clock, hooks, mirror/picture frames, storage boxes; colour accent cushions.

◀ *Modern forged iron bedroom furniture introduces an updated Gothic note to apartment styling. Here its graphic qualities are enhanced by restful blonde wood and wicker, while colour-splash bedlinen and soft furnishings complement the effect.*

▲ **Bold areas of flat colour** – *warm wood tones, green and blue are carefully balanced with soothing white and the neutral shades of metal and glass to create a spacious, restful atmosphere.*

Streamlined wardrobes and shelving units *look good in their own right and are a practical way to organize space and minimize clutter.*

Simple and unfussy, checked bedlinen *provides understated pattern interest in a scheme which relies on plain colours for impact.*

A home study area *is visually at ease in the open-plan bedroom, where the furniture and furnishings are low-key and versatile.*

Sleek and modern task lighting *looks stylish in an apartment-style scheme.*

APARTMENT-STYLE FURNISHINGS

The bedroom furniture should have a light and pleasantly unobtrusive quality and, unlike many conventional bedroom styles, a dual purpose look, so that individual pieces would not seem out of place in a different room. Designs with these adaptable looks are available to suit all budgets, and many are conveniently flat-packed for home assembly. Store clothes and linens, and banish clutter behind doors – in free-standing, streamlined wardrobes or capacious fitted units which utilize alcoves and corners.

The bed may be an updated wrought iron or four poster style, a basic divan with underbed storage, or a sleek model in beech or light wood. Chests of draw-ers, wardrobes and tables can echo these materials, or complement them – pale woods look good with wicker, as does furniture in metal and glass.

◀ *Quirky timepieces are the norm in an Apartment bedroom. The graphic lines of this wiggly stem clock would suit a scheme based on cool neutrals and metallic accents, and make a flattering contrast to warmer woodtones and vibrant colour.*

▲ *The cool, neutral colours of this attic room help maximize the feeling of space and light. Clever touches such as the sliding top-hung doors and the wheel-mounted linen chest underline the contemporary look. The muted green colour accent is supplied by the striped upholstery, window blind and lampshades.*

◀ *A bold colour scheme, simple furnishings and strong contrasts make this an individualist's bedroom. White walls help to maintain the careful colour balance, while green grounds the scheme.*

Apartment-style fabrics

Window treatments play a supporting role in the scheme rather than acting as focal-point furnishings. Wood or metal Venetian blinds, plain Roman and roller-style blinds and tab-headed, threaded-rod or simple gathered curtains are appropriate. Curtain poles in wood or metal may have quirky finials, and tiebacks may be improvised from metal chain, coloured plastic or rope. Typically, fabrics are plain, in cotton sheers, calico or bright colours in cotton or linen mixes. Patterns are usually restricted to graphic checks or stripes and low-key abstracts.

Bedlinen is simple: cotton duvet covers with buttoned or tie details and matching linen, or sheets with bright blankets or throws. White, neutrals, bold solids or modern floral or abstract prints focus on the main colour theme.

In a small, open-plan apartment-style bedroom, colour plays an important role in creating a cohesive whole. Mauve and yellow are natural complementaries, and as such, they work together in a mutually flattering way to create a cosy bedroom area.

Making the most of the sloping wall shape, an expanse of cool blue creates a perfect foil for vivid yellow and white stripe bedlinen. Blonde wood and white walls provide a space-enhancing setting for these colour splashes, and for the carefully balanced touches of accent red.

STYLE DETAILS

Accessories and colour details play an especially important role in the apartment bedroom: the setting is calculatedly simple, and so every addition catches the eye. Aim for a few bold features – a hi-tech table lamp, boldly graphic framed print, or the "architectural" effect of a single specimen flower in a plain glass or metal vase – as these will have far more impact than small groups of objects.

Bedroom furnishings such as large, unusual cushions, laundry containers or innovative storage boxes can conspicuously declare their design credentials. Clever solutions and fun versions of these everyday items are worth showing off and underline the contemporary look.

Looking simple but sophisticated is a feature of apartment style. This wire-frame lamp with its plain cotton shade, and the curvy wooden photo frame are typical stylish accessories.

In a workroom/bedroom, style details play a key role in balancing dual functions. Here, a smartly potted topiary tree is perfectly positioned to bridge the gap, and flatters both areas, as does the pretty but practical window blind and the colour-accent table lamps.

Form and function are appreciated in minimal contemporary interiors, where simple pieces such as this clothes rail blend easily into the scheme.

Bright plastic accessories have a fun here-and-now feel – in tune with apartment-style furnishings. Add a dash of colour to a cool neutral scheme, or top up a colour-splash bedroom with cheerful details such as these clothes hangers.

HARMONIOUS COLOURS

Colours which flow naturally into one another because they are closely related on the colour wheel make for a relaxing and comfortable environment, are easy on the eye and simple to put together.

Harmonious schemes are created using a group of colours which originate from the same area of the colour wheel, rather than from opposite sides. Because the colours are natural neighbours – for example, blues and greens – they blend effortlessly together, offering no jarring contrasts. You can select from a single section of the colour wheel – a range of yellows, for example – to create a monochrome scheme; or choose from two adjacent sections, such as blue and purple; or range even wider, selecting from the greeny yellows, through all the green hues, to the blue-greens. Imagine a landscape of fields and woods in summer – forget-me-not blue sky, fresh green foliage and pale yellow cornfields. Placed on the colour wheel, you can see that the colours are closely related, so the whole blend is pleasant on the eye.

> *Glass goblets in adjacent harmonies – blue-green, through pure blue to amethyst – would look perfectly at home in the room below. The subtle play of light on the glass is a tonal bonus.*

> *Harmonious schemes often surprise with their unusual yet highly successful colour combinations – as in this sitting room, where cool aqua provides a striking backdrop for a soft-toned violet sofa. Scarlet roses and a mellow scarlet and gold cushion provide warm neighbouring accents.*

For a sunny outlook all year round, base a room scheme entirely on the adjacent warm colours of the spectrum – from the saffron yellow of the sofa fabric, through the sun-bleached terracotta of the crockery and scatter cushion, to the hot pinks of the walls, lampshade and footstool. Softer shades, such as the pale pink of the small cushion and painted chair, add tonal interest.

These vibrant hues, ranging between yellow and red on the colour wheel, can be used to create a warm, energetic scheme, as in the living room shown above.

ADJACENT SCHEMES

Typical harmonious schemes are based on hues which sit together between two of the three primary colours – red, blue and yellow – on the colour wheel. The hues between yellow and red cover the earthy, natural pigments of terracotta, burnt orange and ochre yellows to give a warm, vibrantly sunny scheme. Ranging between red and blue gives a rich, noble palette of crimson, burgundy, purple and violet; while the cool side of the spectrum runs between blue and yellow, from tranquil turquoise and aqua, through all the lush greens to citrus lime and lemon.

Choosing colours from either side of a primary colour – for example purple, through blue to jade green, or from the sharp tones of lime green, through chrome yellow to yellow-orange – can still make a harmonious scheme, but they need careful planning as they are naturally discordant. Softening one or two of the colours with white into a pastel tint, or smudging them towards a greyish shade, can smooth the transition and add a calming note.

COLOUR ACCENTS

One of the pitfalls of harmonious schemes is a tendency to monotony, as all the colours blend so well together. You can easily correct this with accents – small splashes of colour introduced around the room, perhaps in a vase, a plant, a few cushions or a picture – which come from a different part of the spectrum.

Contrast accents In adjacent harmony schemes placed firmly in either the cool or warm side of the spectrum, accenting with a colour from the opposite side adds a dash of contrast, and balances the temperature nicely. A warm blend of pinks and berry reds can seem a little stifling on a brilliant summer day: balance the effect with fresh touches of spring green in houseplants, a floral pattern with big verdant leaves, or a collection of jade green ornaments grouped on the mantelpiece. Alternatively, you can take the chill off a cool green and blue scheme, without losing the airy, outdoor feel, by adding large terracotta pots for plants, a huge bowl of glowing oranges or a creamy yellow flower display.

Neighbouring accents In monochromatic schemes, choose a hue from one of the close neighbours on the spectrum, rather than anything too strongly contrasting: invigorate a peaceful green bedroom by scattering some turquoise silk cushions on the bed, and standing a matching fabric-covered picture frame on the dressing table. Likewise, a warm yellow or pink monochrome scheme would benefit from soft orange accents.

Contrast accents of mid green in the picture mounts and fresh foliage, and of cool blue on the painted chest of drawers and table cloth print, add interest and balance to this warm pink and peachy scheme.

Chalky pastel yellow stripes add a warming contrast accent to this cool aqua bathroom. Turquoise and marine blue add deeper notes, vital to creating a good tonal balance.

BLACK DEFINITION

Black adds a spark unlike any other colour, and some say that no room is complete without it. A narrow black lacquered picture frame, or a pair of wrought iron candlesticks on a dining table, bring a sober touch of elegance and a snap of contrast to many schemes. One example enjoying a popular revival is the Georgian print room, where black and white prints make a graphic impact against vibrant yellow or rich terracotta walls.

In a harmonious contemporary scheme, perhaps based on a blend of citrus tones in exuberant yellows and limes, sharp black details, such as spiky lamps and sound equipment, provide a serious, functional note.

Another favourite in this field is a black and white chequered floor which gives a crisp, graphic grounding for other more lively colours – a hallway, perhaps, decorated in warm tones of terracotta and burnt orange, or a conservatory in rich mixtures of green.

➤ *A restful bedroom scheme based on cool blues and greens is given definition by the curving lines of a distinctive iron bedstead, and a pair of spiky bedside tables.*

▼ *An elegant glass and wrought iron dining table with matching chairs adds snappy contrast and a contemporary note to this rich red and gold scheme.*

A cream sofa provides a neutral backdrop for the gentle, warm tones of pale yellow, peach and pink cushions, letting the eye focus on their subtle blend of colour and pattern.

Vivid furnishings in bright blue and lime green, with acid yellow accessories providing a sharp accent, take centre stage against a quiet background of cream paintwork. A pale wood floor and furniture are welcome warming influences.

NEUTRAL BACKGROUNDS

Many classic combinations are based on a harmonious grouping of colours, highlighted or backed up with neutral tones. The intricate and detailed designs of willow pattern china rely on a single shade of rich blue set against a background of white or cream, and this duo forms the foundation of an endlessly successful room scheme: set a range of blues, in plains, patterns and textures, against white, cream and beige for a pure, clean and fresh looking room, balanced by the warm tones of natural wood and basket-

ware. Work the same formula around rich hot reds, where cool beiges and fawns allow the strong, warm tones to glow out against their softer, receding backdrop.

Bear in mind that different woods have very different colourings, and should be chosen accordingly as part of the scheme: ash is a cool, silvery beige, while oak has warm, golden hues, and cherry a reddish glow. Use them to add touches of contrast to harmonious schemes, or to blend effortlessly.

PATTERN AND TEXTURE

The interest provided by patterns and textures is an important part of building a colour scheme – especially a harmonious scheme.

To create a lively touch in a quiet scheme, include patterns of varying sizes – perhaps a large check, a medium-sized floral motif, and a tiny sprig, so there is interest at each focal range. For contemporary impact in a room of plain, blended colours, introduce one strong, large-scale pattern incorporating most of the colours in the scheme – say a large modern print for Roman blinds, or a boldly patterned throw on a sofa. Use patterns to define particular areas in a room – a vigorously patterned rug creating a pool of colour around the dining table and chairs, for example.

Achieving a satisfying combination of textures is another route to an interesting harmonious scheme. Every surface has character in its texture: wood can be buffed to a glossy polish or distressed for a rough, rustic look; floors can be luxuriously carpeted, scratchily textured with jute matting, or laid with cool, smooth floor tiles; fabrics, too, offer a huge range of textural effects.

▼ *Gentle green and yellow harmonies are given a lift with subtle pattern and texture details, and neutral wood and wicker tones.*

▶ *In this green and yellow scheme, broken colour paint effects create a lively balance with the boldly patterned fabrics.*

CONTRAST COLOURS

*Colour is a powerful decorating tool, and contrast colour schemes –
created with a combination of hues from the warm and cool side of the
colour wheel – are always the most dynamic.*

Contrast colours are an exciting visual balancing act, one that occurs in nature all the time: think of golden sand lapped by a sparkling blue sea, a green meadow dotted with scarlet poppies, or a carpet of purple and yellow crocuses.

Nature's brilliant examples may seem unnerving and a hard act to follow in decorating terms, but some of the most successful schemes use contrasts in varying degrees for their impact. Contrast colours have an energy that can be lacking in "safer" schemes based around harmonies

and monochromes. So by being adventurous and choosing contrasts, you can use their invigorating qualities to good effect – especially in an active area such as a hallway, dining room, kitchen or playroom, where a lively colour scheme is appropriate.

You can make contrast colours the base for a room scheme, or use them sparingly in brilliant bursts, set against neutrals and harmonies, to add stimulating colour notes to quieter schemes. Brighten a cool room by adding warm-toned accessories, or introduce calming touches of cooler

colour to a sunny room. When tinted with white, toned-down contrasts become easy-on-the eye pastels; when darkened with black, they soften into muted shades – contrast colours give you so many options.

▼ *Soft green and orange furnishings set against a neutral background show how a contrast colour gives energy to a scheme.*

SOFTENED CONTRASTS

Contrast schemes depend on a good tonal balance to work successfully. An accepted approach is to use a larger expanse of one colour – usually the cool colour – balanced by smaller amounts and varying tones of the warm colour. This can work equally well in reverse, with a mainly warm scheme – especially in a cold room, or where a cosy atmosphere is a priority.

Used in equal amounts, contrast colours can be startling: red and green, for example, share the same tonal value so they dazzle the eye when placed together. To live comfortably with these colours, one or other of them has to be used sparingly, or considerably reduced in intensity, as in the softened pale green and red scheme on page 55 (*bottom*).

Blue and purple are tonally darker than contrasting yellow, lime or orange, so these hues start with an easier visual balance. Even so, softening their intensities or rationing their use in a room makes them a less formidable option. For example, the soft mauve and pale lime scheme, tempered by gentle green, shown on page 55 (*top*), makes an individualistic colour statement, but the gentle tints are a far cry from the original full-strength purple and lime green of the colour wheel.

◄ *Blue and yellow are classic contrasts. By shifting slightly round the colour wheel both colours here have a warm cast. Golden yellow provides a background for the mid blue sofa and detail interest in the cushions, while blue pattern accents carry the eye round the room.*

► *Contrast accents liven up a colour scheme based on gentle harmonies. Accessories in warm mauve and cool lime create a stylish splash in this sitting room.*

Ready-made contrasts

Many fabric and wallpaper designs and coordinated furnishing ranges are based on contrast colours, but often the hues are so softened that this may not be immediately noticeable. If you are unsure how to start planning a contrast scheme, it is well worth looking at these ready-made designs. Choose an example you like and note how the colours balance; see how they are used in proportion to one another, and how texture or pattern alters their tonal values.

▶ *This gentle, light-enhanced scheme in pale lime and mauve conjures up the fragility of new leaf shoots and delicate flowerbuds. Traditional print fabrics provide an interesting twist in this essentially modern scheme.*

▼ *Warm terracotta provides a subtle background for muted blue contrast accents in this nursery. Different tonal values of both colours add depth and textural interest to the scheme.*

▼ *Broken paint effects and fabric prints are a perfect way to soften intense hues. Here, a diffused green background creates a cool contrast with the red and white chair covers.*

BOLD CONTRASTS

Taking the first steps to creating a vivid, boldly contrasting scheme can require strong resolve, especially if you are not used to living with stronger colours. Seeing the play of warm and cool hues, and how they can revitalize a room, persuades many to opt for this more individual approach. Lively contrasts create instant atmosphere; a hall or dining room in an advancing, warm colour tempered with contrast accents immediately conveys a welcoming or dramatic atmosphere. Likewise, more offbeat contrasts, such as the lime

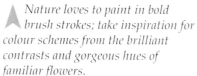

▼ *The ultimate in bold contrasts, this jewel-rich bedroom shows a dramatic commitment to colour. Pure white bedlinen and a deep blue lampshade add further flamboyant touches.*

▲ *Nature loves to paint in bold brush strokes; take inspiration for colour schemes from the brilliant contrasts and gorgeous hues of familiar flowers.*

green and purple scheme shown on page 57 (*bottom*), or a glowing ginger scheme teamed with turquoise or purple, create strong contemporary style statements.

Balancing contrasts

Playing one strong colour off against another is the attraction and challenge in bolder schemes. As the warm, advancing, and cool, receding qualities of colours are more noticeable in bold contrasts, their effects have more impact.

Achieving the right tonal balance is vital if you are to avoid an unsettling visual dual. Successful ways to tame bold contrasts include reducing the intensity of one of the colours, or using a greater proportion of one colour, balanced with smaller amounts of contrast colour. You can hold a bold scheme together and give it a lift by blending in different tones of the main colour; and by introducing other bold colours in smaller amounts, as shown in the sumptuous red and green bedroom on the left, where the blue bedside lamp is a vibrant finishing touch.

To acclimatize yourself to bold contrasts, try using them as accents in harmonious or low-key schemes. Besides spicing up a room, boldly coloured accessories are a quick way to introduce seasonal colour changes.

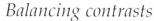

Pattern and texture

A useful way to integrate bold contrast colours in a scheme is with pattern and texture. Little touches of colour in varied tones carried through a scheme help balance the overall effect.

Floral prints, checks and stripes, crunchy weaves and shiny surfaces in varied tonal combinations of the main contrast colours all have a part to play in a bold scheme. They perform a vital balancing act, helping to create a cohesive whole.

This vibrant yellow dining room shows how a warm, advancing colour needs only a touch of complementary blue to balance the effect.

Purple and lime strike a stylish contemporary note in this dramatically simple sitting room, where the tonal balance is beautifully fine-tuned. The bold blue rug grounds the sofa and chair and is a flattering contrast.

A table setting provides an ideal opportunity to introduce bold accents to a quieter scheme.

CONTRASTS WITH NEUTRALS

Neutrals provide a wonderful blank canvas for contrast colour statements. Whether your soft furnishings are in softly contrasting colours against sparkling white walls, or the effect is reversed with dramatic colour-splashed walls and neutral furniture and furnishings, neutrals really flatter contrasts used in any strength.

Combining contrasts with neutrals can be a first step to gaining confidence in using colour. The contrast colours can be limited to a group of cushions on a neutral sofa, perhaps picking up colours from a picture or rug, or concentrated in a vibrant curtain print on a neutral background. Alternatively, you may simply opt for a dramatic flower display in nature's own inspiring contrast colours.

Traditional style furnishings are given a modern twist with cool blue and hot pink. Clear white and soft fawn neutrals are a perfect foil for the beautifully balanced colours and patterns.

Neutral walls and upholstery provide an ideal setting for bold contrast accessories. Here, balanced tones of blue, yellow, ochre and terracotta add colour to a soft modern sitting room.

Two sizes of picture mats compensate for the tonal difference between orange and blue. This adjustment balances the pair against their flattering neutral background.

Neutrals can bring out the best in many contrast colour schemes. Here, clear white enhances the timeless appeal of fresh green and pink.

COLOUR ACCENTS

*Chosen with care, one or two colourful accessories can lift
the mood of a whole room, providing a focal point and bringing
lively interest into an otherwise bland colour scheme.*

One of the most common problems encountered when refurbishing a room is how to create a flexible, easy-to-live-with setting. You may be uncertain of your colour preferences and reluctant to commit yourself to strong colours. This often means choosing furnishings, colours and fabrics that don't tie you to a particular look – but it can also result in a lifeless, low-key room which can actually have a negative effect on your state of mind.

Neutral schemes using safe shades of beige and cream or grey often fall into the lifeless category, but a dull

scheme may also be the result of colour coordinating too thoroughly – an entire room decorated in varying shades of blue, for instance, can end up looking cool and restful to the point of boredom.

By injecting splashes of contrasting colour in small but significant areas – inexpensive accessories such as cushions, lampshades, a vase of flowers – you can quickly and easily bring a dull scheme to life. It is a much less nerve-racking process than changing the wall colour or a big item such as curtains, as you can bring home a small item to test *in situ*

without a large outlay. You can even use something you already have in the house – for example, move a bowl of lemons from the kitchen to a bedside table to see what effect splashes of citrus yellow would have in a moody blue bedroom.

A brightly coloured picture on the wall sets the theme for a series of zingy lime green accent touches, which bring to life the aqua tones of this huge kitchen dresser. Natural basketware, wood and terracotta soften the impact.

COLOUR WHEEL MAGIC

To be sure that you create the effect you want with accent colours, go back to the basics of the colour wheel. You can highlight a monochromatic room scheme – one which uses a range of greens, for example – by picking one or two colours from the sections directly next to green – blue and yellow – on the colour wheel. Many of the most pleasant and relaxing schemes are created in this way.

The further you move round the colour wheel from your main colour,

the greater the contrast, so a splash of red pottery or glass in a predominantly blue room will catch the eye irresistibly; if you prefer softer colours, you can work the same trick with a delicate touch by setting pastel pinks against cool pale blues.

To create a real sense of energy, add flashes of colour from the range directly opposite the main room colour on the wheel – spicy reds and oranges against deep bottle greens, or violet to warm up lime green.

▼ *Accent colours don't have to be strong and bright. Here, delicate pink provides soft colour accents for the cool aquatint of the wall stripes. Pink adds a warming accent to the whole scheme without being overpowering.*

▶ *The bold daubs of red in the pieces of studio glass almost vibrate against the saturated blue of the wall behind: the simple forms of contemporary furniture allow confident colour combinations to take centre stage.*

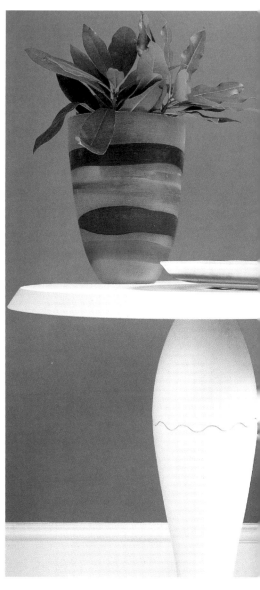

▶ *A single fiery red gerbera flames against the knocked-back blue of a bookcase, cleverly pointing up the russet and gold tones of a row of antique books. The gilding is picked up again in the delicate metallic finish of the dainty glassware.*

Accent Highlights

If you have a scheme that already combines a pair of complementary colours – perhaps apricot and pistachio green – in a range of patterns, you can simply intensify the existing tones and use them in solid blocks of colour to accent the scheme. For example, make up a clutch of cushions using patterned fabrics mixed with plain ones in deeper shades of apricot and green. Add plain borders to curtains or blinds, and pile a green bowl with oranges to carry the point through.

▶ *Without the solid blocks of deeper plain colour in the cushions and curtain borders, this room could lack definition. Deepening the main colours and using them as accents pulls the whole scheme together and gives it focus.*

▼ *Once you have painted your bathroom in hot orange and raspberry, lime green towels may seem quite tame – but in fact they add a welcome cooling touch to the sizzle of the wall colours, absorbing some of the heat.*

ACCENTING NEUTRALS

When you tire of the uniformity of creamy walls, sensible beige fabrics and natural finishes, there are all sorts of ways to spark up the look. Before branching out into full colour, consider other neutrals such as charcoal, black and chestnut brown and focus on textural interest with accessories in cast or wrought iron, ebony-effect wood or dark wool-blend fabrics. All shades of green make natural partners for neutral schemes to give them a gentle lift.

For some livelier colour, try burnt orange and russet, blended in an ethnic throw or raw silk cushions. Most warm or deep colours work well against neutrals – place a collection of modern glass pieces or old bottles in jewel colours, to catch the light, or cover a chair in a rich indigo and add patterned cushions on the sofa that pick up the colour.

Monochromatic schemes of graphic black and white are effective but sometimes too stark to live with until you drop in just one touch of colour – a brilliant fuchsia silk cushion, a lime green lampshade or perhaps a single orange flower.

Individual and inventive, a crisp black and white theme here gives an almost cell-like serenity to a bedroom, lightened by the seductively rich tones of the deep aqua green bedlinen, which centres attention firmly on the bed.

Neutral accents

Strong colours used in large areas can sometimes be overpowering, or even lose some of their potential because of a lack of contrast. You can "anchor" a strong colour scheme and flatter it at the same time with the severe neutrality of black and white. Try the effect of a black and white check against a rich ochre yellow wall or electric blue sofa. Deep rich browns have the same effect: carved polished wood boxes or trays, ethnic artifacts and basketware with an antiqued varnish all add interest to bland schemes, and are especially effective in giving depth to pale pastels such as aqua or powder blue.

◀ *The elegant and restrained decoration of this dining room makes the most of its architectural features and abundance of light. But it is the careful introduction of accent shades of green in the chair covers, candles, flowers and wreath which give it character and style.*

◀ *A geometric black and white patterned frame adds sharp accent detail in this green and blue scheme. The colours in the zebra picture link together the green wall and blue chest, while the zebra theme is carried through to the lampshade.*

◀ *Graphic black and white adds emphasis to the straight lines in this entrance hall – the zigzag lines of the stairs, the Venetian blind and the simple door. A vibrant fuchsia accent cushion highlights the rounded lines of the chair, the rug design and the intriguing sculpture.*

PLACING ACCENTS

Draw attention to attractive features in your room with colour accents – place a colourful painting on the chimney breast to draw attention to a marble fireplace, or march a row of single flowers in individual vases along the sill of a sunny window.

Using colour accents, you can lead the eye round the room with a continous trail of interest, varying the size of the accessory, and even the colour, to keep up a satisfying rhythm. For example, if you are accenting a blue room with citrus shades, use lemon for a big bowl on a coffee table, then link this to the sofa with a lemon and lime checked throw. A lime green vase on a windowsill continues the theme.

◄ *A line of cheery yellow gerberas fixes attention firmly at the window, making the most of the happy combination of blue and yellow. Placing flowers singly like this strings out the accent colour to emphasize the window.*

▲ *Spots of spiky orange lead the eye irresistibly round the room without overpowering the fresh yellows and leafy greens. Orange is a natural accent choice as it lies next to yellow on the colour wheel; blue, coming directly next to green, would be equally effective but cooler.*

◄ *The vibrant dazzle of a single red cushion ensures that you don't miss the sweeping contemporary lines of the sofa on which it sits. Colour accent cushions and throws are perfect for highlighting a favourite piece of furniture.*

COLOUR BRIGHTS

*Be bold and drench a room with vibrant colour – or try its
powerful effects in smaller splashes. Colour brights may not be
for the faint-hearted, but they certainly inspire confidence.*

I f you have only ever decorated with pale colours and
neutrals, taking the plunge with a bold colour scheme
can take a little nerve. Once you realize the impressive
effects you can achieve, a whole new approach to colour
scheming opens up.

Colour brights have a strong contemporary feel. The
term describes a fresh, lively way of decorating with a
vibrant palette of primary colours, rich muted shades and
sharp pastels. You can turn colour into a style statement,
create and define a sense of space, describe a mood, or use
it as a potent, versatile accessory.

Whether the effect you want to create is intimate, warm

*Jewel bright colours create the kind of warm and intimate
atmosphere that is well suited to a dining room. The
boldly patterned coordinated fabrics combine all the main
colours in the scheme, which together with neutrals, play a
crucial part in balancing the finished effect.*

and welcoming, or more dramatic – from sumptuous to
restrained minimalism – decorating with well-balanced,
gloriously bright colour combinations brings its rewards.
The results are a revitalized home, refreshed with colour
that expresses your true personality.

WORKING WITH COLOUR BRIGHTS

Using vibrant colours in a scheme isn't a new idea. Many grand houses of the past made extravagant and innovative use of bright shades. Zinging acid yellows, deep fuchsias and purples, rich royal blues and emerald greens all provided fabulous backdrops and dramatically rich furnishings to complement ornate period architecture and furniture.

In modern terms, these colours are still a major influence, but it is the way you can use them to enhance present-day interiors, and to create streamlined up-to-date schemes that makes them particularly interesting. The glowing jewel colours seen in the sumptuous brocades and silks of the past are now joined by modern synthetics – strong, hi-tech pastels, vivid acid brights and resonating spice tones. Use them together in exciting combinations: as brilliant harmonies – energizing poppy red, cinnamon and mustard yellow, for example – and as unusual contrasts; flatter pared-down, contemporary-style pale wood furniture with a shimmering turquoise and muted tangerine or lime scheme. You can also set colour brights very successfully against a bold expanse of white or neutral shades, and flatter them with the subtle sheen of metallic accents.

◄ *Vivid tropical orange "draws in" the walls to create a close, vibrant space. This is tempered by the cooler splashes of fruity yellow and green in the bright and cheerful flower prints, which also introduce a welcome visual change of pace.*

Tropical colours are the ultimate in colour brights. Lush tones of lime green, yellow and glowing orange echo one another, to create a well-balanced scheme. Pale upholstery creates a visual breathing space, and dark-toned foliage adds a deeper accent.

Defining Space with Colour

Think in broad terms and use vigorous colour combinations to define the shapes in the room. Use bold colours to accentuate proportions, to define features and divide areas that lead into one another. This works well if the colours you use balance tonally, and you avoid harsh contrasts.

Help to create a visual link between different colour areas by flowing a new toning colour or neutral throughout – perhaps for ceilings, woodwork, or for furnishings and accessories. Chair and picture rails are also ideal conduits for these "go-between" colours.

For an easy transition between adjoining rooms – perhaps a living room to hall – and to highlight areas of different activity within a room, choose colours from adjacent sections of the colour wheel, from either the warm or cool side.

For greater definition, try balancing a mix of contrast colours and link them with another shade to help colour flow. Take architectural features such as an alcove, trimwork, a window or door wall, or a large piece of furniture as the natural start of a colour break on walls. Alternatively, limit a contrast colour to smaller features such as trims, skirting, window and door frames.

Using a restrained palette of colour brights, cool lemon yellow seems to bathe the space with light. Along with neutrals, touches of turquoise, blue and coral pink add exciting accents in this minimal scheme.

COLOUR BLOCKS AND PATTERNS

A rewarding aspect of colour brights is that however you use them they create an impact. You can saturate a room with rich harmonies, bathe it in subtle contrasts, or just use sparky colour accents against a backdrop of neutrals, and the colours glow and make their vital presence felt.

Because of their high profile, it is important to achieve a well-balanced scheme, and this is where pattern can help. When you combine colour brights in a room, even plain colours start to create pattern formations. These patterns may be formed by the simple repetition of colour blocks – a bright sofa and chairs against contrast walls, for example, or a row of colourful cushions or picture frames. Hold the look together by introducing the same colours again – as accents throughout the room in soft furnishings and carefully grouped accessories.

Many new coordinating ranges have a colour bright theme. They provide ready-made pattern options, so that balancing strong colour effects is made easy. You can choose a fabric print for curtains or upholstery which incorporates all the colours used elsewhere in plain, bold blocks, knowing that the overall effect will be successful.

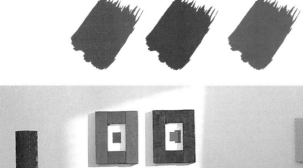

This abstract patterned rug is a brilliant addition here – it is interesting in its own right, and the colours balance perfectly with the seating and accessories.

Clever colour blocking creates a vivid scheme where a pale background provides a soft contrast for super-rich crimson and harmonizing purple. The dramatic sofa and chair are carefully balanced by the matching and complementary accents elsewhere in the room.

Hot and spicy brights can be overpowering, but a visual break with brilliant red and white checks relieves the heat. The colours all flow beautifully throughout the scheme, showing how important it is to establish colour links with an adjacent room.

A splash of shocking pink is cleverly balanced by a bright blue china display and vivid little colour details.

BRIGHT ACCENTS

As hot tropical pastels and stronger brews, some colour brights seem bathed in sunshine, with a clarity and intensity that creates a cheerful atmosphere wherever you use them. This light-enhanced quality makes bright pink, lush green, vibrant orange, lemon and lime a natural choice for colour accents in schemes based on lighter toning shades and pale neutrals.

Other brights have deeper, jewel-like qualities – primaries red, yellow and blue, royal purple, crimson, deep turquoise and emerald green. This dramatic colour group needs some restraint to create a good balance. You can offset an expanse of strong colour with a group of complementary accents, and use one or more intense brights to put a punch in a mainly white scheme.

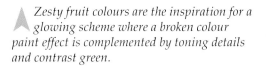

Accessories provide a quick way to give a scheme a new slant, or a major colour boost. Versatile jewel colours look magnificent with other rich colours, and give a lift to neutral schemes.

Zesty fruit colours are the inspiration for a glowing scheme where a broken colour paint effect is complemented by toning details and contrast green.

Patterns in brilliant carnival colours are popular with most young children. Use them as furnishings and accessories to jolly up a scheme based on matching or toning plains and white.

Hot mustard yellow defines this dresser in a way no other colour can. Set in an otherwise neutral scheme, its dramatic impact is assured.

PURPLE AND GREEN

Combine shades of grape, lime and lavender for lively, unexpected schemes that are easy and restful to live with. From wildly quirky to subtle and soothing, purple and green make a versatile and inspiring duo.

Situated at each end of the cool spectrum, purple and green offer a wide palette of hues which are well worth exploring for a new scheme. Deep acid purple had its heyday in the sixties and seventies, but in recent times it has resurfaced in a delicious range of flowery and fruity shades: dreamy hyacinth blue, pale dewy lilac and vivid lavender are ranged with dark and subtle shades of grape, damson and plum.

Take inspiration from nature and set these tantalizing shades against some of the myriad shades of leafy green for the perfect complement: look round your garden, or take a country walk, to see how the silver-green of the lavender bush flatters its spikes of mauve, or the contrast of fresh, new, heart-shaped leaves against the froth of lilac blossom. Try a brilliant grass green cushion on a chair covered in murky damson purple, or blend almond green or subtle olive walls with a pale violet patterned print for a light and elegant springtime look.

A harmonious blend of fruit and leafy tones, verdigris and recycled glass is interpreted in the plaid wool, ageing paint and pleated paper in this display.

In a sophisticated bathroom scheme where period style meets pared-down contemporary looks, soft lavender and lime create a delicate colour balance. Enhanced by ornate gilt accents, the effect is appealingly romantic.

Fresh, spring-like shades of almond and lavender are spiked with white for a crisp and cool but essentially pretty look. Keep furnishings simple and unfussy, adding plenty of living colour with plants and flowers – here, box trees and globular heads of hydrangea.

Soft and Gentle

As the shades of purple and green are all mainly cool, the lighter shades can be used to create an airy, open look, but without being chilly. The combination is ideal for the fresh, outdoors feel popular in today's homes, and works well with natural finishes, wood floors and simple modern furnishings.

Many of the lighter shades of green make a calming and peaceful background for busy lives. Try a translucent wash of light apple green over an off-white base, or pick a soft jade green and emphasize it with a stronger tone for woodwork. You could pick up this deeper shade for upholstery, and bring in a delicate lavender for curtains and cushions, using simple plain or check fabrics with a few floral touches.

Alternatively, reverse the colours and coat the walls in a flat layer of pale mauve or hyacinth blue for a modern but pretty effect, perhaps in a guest bedroom. Add fresh, leafy green accessories – bedlinen, a painted bedside table – as a contrast. Leaf prints are a popular theme in fabrics, and make interesting curtains or blinds. Pale blonde wood, limed oak or cane furniture keeps the mood suitably light and relaxed.

PERIOD CHARM

For a more formal effect, hark back to the whimsical look of seventeenth-century France with elegant tones of greenish-grey and lilac in beaded panels on the walls, and huge gilt-framed mirrors to bounce the light round the room. Hunt out toile de Jouy in green or violet for curtains, and make up bolsters and cushions in shiny brocades to soften slender-legged chaises longues and chairs.

These pretty but fresh colours bring a new lease of life to the country cottage look, too. Their light tones form a flattering backdrop to age-burnished wood, dainty china and flowery prints, and you will find plenty of pretty fabrics and papers smothered in wisteria, lilac or violet sprigs.

Muted greyish purples set against soft green walls give a totally different slant to country style design. Combined with simple creamy drapes and touches of soft red for warmth, the colour scheme brings life to old, comfortable furniture and treasured ornaments.

Inspiration from nature again creates a gentle combination based on apple green and lilac. The detailed wall panelling is washed in translucent colour, with beading picked out in soft pale violet. Cushion accessories pick up these subtle tones.

SHARP CONTRASTS

If you prefer a confident, contemporary mood, choose from the more intense versions of purple and green to create an up-to-the-minute look. Set tangy lime against deep royal purple or an intense lavender, or try sharp apple green against a rich damson; there are far more of these colours about, in fabrics, wallpapers and accessories. Look for the new vogue in vegetable prints, featuring splashily painted eggplants with gleaming purple skins, alongside brilliant green lettuces and green and purple cabbages. Try using one of these prints as a simple panel at the window, then use the colours from it as a theme for the room in bold blocks – a sculptured curvy sofa in deep violet velvet with one huge cushion in bright green, set against plain white walls and graphic black and white accessories.

For a fresh, lively bedroom, choose these colours in boldly checked bedlinen and throws. Coordinate the bright and fresh theme by washing the walls in flat planes of colour – perhaps two or three toning shades of mauve,

Relieved by liberal splashes of refreshing white, rich violet and lilac-mauves blend with cooler blue details in this fun range of bedroom coordinates. The vitality of the graphic designs is complemented by acid green which, as a simple colour accent, adds a vital spark to the scheme.

hyacinth and lavender, all very calm and soothing colours. Spark the theme up with flashes of viridian or grape green – on, for example, lamp-shades, a mirror frame, or a fluffy cotton rug on a pale wood floor.

Small areas in a bathroom can take on an exciting contemporary zing with confident slabs of bold colour. You could paint the walls a tangy lemony lime, for instance, using tiles of a similar but slightly greener shade. Add stainless steel fittings and lush lavender towels, bottles of purple bath oil and violet soap. Look out for sophisticated plastic accessories too, which pick up these fun colours.

The strength and liveliness of the purple and green theme make it an ideal candidate for adding splashes of it to a cool, modern interior in pale neutral shades. Take your inspiration from nature – fill an emerald green bowl with dusky violet damsons, or mix purple delphiniums and lime green "Bells of Ireland" in a tall lilac vase.

◀ *Vibrant and exciting, an intense shade of lavender floods the walls and curtains (above) of this bedroom with colour, throwing the lime of the peg rail, curtain pole and chair into sizzling contrast. For a casual combination of upbeat colour, blues, greens and yellows are mixed together on the bed, freshened with plenty of white.*

▶ *Take inspiration from the vibrant purples and greens of flowering shrubs. Here, the intricate surface detailing of a screen is picked out and highlighted with a subtle paint effect in rich green. The dramatic purple cushion adds a flash of brilliant colour.*

◀ *A flourish of painted lavender feathers on a plate sets off the gleaming green of crisp apples beautifully.*

HEATHERY MIXES

If your taste is for more muted, earthy shades and a comfortable, traditional style, take your inspiration from the heathers and mosses of the Scottish glens: subtle, quiet colours that blend well with dark woods, warm woolly textures and worn grey stone. This is an unusual but attractive scheme, and can be stretched to include soft mauve-pinks, deep fir green and misty greys and beiges. Tweedy mixes make sturdy upholstery covers, and tartans in misty mountain blues and greens feature as throws or even curtains. Gentle greens such as lovat and olive are good for carpets and spriggy wallpapers. Fill silver bowls with heather or thistles, and grow ornamental pink and purple cabbages for winter colour on a windowsill.

Subtle lichen greens, in a sprigged wallpaper and velvet sofa upholstery, make a quiet backdrop for a heathery mix of lilac and pink in cushions and plaids. The effect is a comfortable and welcoming living room.

A riot of purples and pinks in a herbaceoous border (top) is cooled by the lush greens of the surrounding foliage. Images like this, and the frivolous purple-pink in the ornamental cabbage (above) can be used as ready-made colour swatches for warm and restful schemes.

Giant dried thistle heads pushed into a twist of tartan make suitably casual tiebacks for the rich forest green of the tartan curtains. The pale mauve of the thistles blends perfectly with the more heathery shade of the paintwork.

BLUE AND YELLOW

Yellow is a happy, enlivening colour; blue is more contemplative and restful. When combined, their various shades and hues offer a whole host of exciting decorating possibilities.

Blue and yellow, when combined, form a favourite interior colour scheme; thus there is an amazing range of furnishing fabrics, wallpapers and paint shades to choose from. Yet creating a successful scheme takes some thought, as the hues and tones of the two colours can be teamed in an almost infinite number of ways to create quite radically different effects.

Yellow is traditionally thought of as a warm, sunny colour, while blue is cool. Yet there are cool yellows and warm blues; lemon and winter jasmine are cool, while ultramarine and violet-blues tend to be warm. Acid yellows won't look right in a soft bedroom scheme, while warmer lilac blues often jar in clean, modern rooms.

Just as sunny yellows serve to liven colder blues, the sharp acid tones of some yellows complement warm blue shades. Nature provides pointers to successful blue/yellow combinations:

An earthy yellow combines with a deep china blue to form a sophisticated scheme. The wall colour is intensified by a clever choice of lighting, which gives extra depth to the paint surface.

the aquamarine of the sea and the light, bright yellow of sand; the cobalt blue of a summer sky and the slightly dulled, warm yellow of a ripe field of corn; the intense violet-blue of irises with the sharp lemon of their stamens.

SOLID COMBINATIONS

Success with solid areas of blue and yellow depends on the right choice of shades – seeking them out is well worth the effort as results can be rewarding and are often quite dramatic. If you are starting from scratch, cut patches of coloured paper from magazines or catalogues and try them out against each other. Team swatches of fabric, or study combinations on paint charts until you find the shades you like. Bear in mind, too, that the colours will alter slightly depending on the light and orientation of your room – if choosing paint for walls, test it using a matchpot, even if you just paint a sheet of paper and hold it in place. The colour may appear to change considerably.

Once you have found your principal blue and yellow, establish a hierarchy – two colours used in exactly the same quantities will not usually sit comfortably. Start with your main colour and introduce the second colour as an accent.

You can achieve the boldest effects by balancing large areas of one colour – the floor for example – against a large area of another colour, such as the wall. Consider first, though, the dimensions of your room; dark, dominant colours on the walls will draw them in, giving an intimate feel, while painting them with the lighter of the two shades will create a more open, expansive look.

▲ *Coloured lampshades are an extremely effective way of bringing colour into a room. Even the smallest lights, such as these chrome-plated candle lamps, can have an enormous effect on the colour of your night time scheme.*

▶ *The mood of this scheme is sunny but restful, making it a perfect choice for a bedroom. Custard yellow is teamed with a chalky cobalt, used in the deep window recess where it picks up the colour of the sky. Cool primrose yellow and the dark blue of the fabrics complete the scheme.*

This strong, contemporary living room uses lemon with a hint of white for the walls – the overall effect is cool but not cold – and its paleness serves to open out the room. The intense blue of the upholstery is jewel-like – the colour of the twilight summer sky – and serves to accentuate the dominance of the welcoming seating.

Blue is a popular choice for bathrooms, and here, deep cobalt blue provides the accent on towels, fabric and tiles. The sunny yellow of the walls is carried through the chequered theme of the room, and is used in a deeper shade on the floor, and more mutedly on the smart fabric shower curtain.

PATTERN FOR DRAMA

Adding pattern to your colour combination can alter the feel of the scheme quite considerably. Although the colours you choose, when seen on their own, might be fresh and bold, the effect of yellow on blue (or vice versa) is often strikingly dramatic. The smaller the pattern, the more the two colours blend in the eye, creating a new, more subtle shade. For dramatic statements, choose loud patterns with colours which are contrasting in tone – deep indigo blues with patterns of rich yellow gold, for example, or strong blue and yellow stripes stamped with scrolls and swirls in lighter shades. Yellow ochre, when used on certain furnishing fabrics has a distinctly golden feel, which teams well with dazzling lapis lazuli.

When decorating with patterned yellows and blues, begin with the pattern colours and allow them to lead your scheme. Choose softer versions of the same colours for the paintwork, and choose a floorcovering that doesn't fight with the furnishing or wallcovering design.

Several shades of blue and yellow are elegantly combined in this softly opulent sitting room. Gold, cream and pale ochre are complemented by soft pastel blue, with hints of sky blue providing accents on the furnishing fabric.

Differing patterns in the same blue and yellow shades are the feature in this exotic, faintly eastern-style room. Muted ochre and sapphire blue are teamed to their best advantage, and the colourway is accentuated by the understated treatment of the walls and floorcovering.

SUBTLE ELEGANCE

Muted tones of blue and yellow are the easiest of all to live with. Whether used as plains on walls and floors, or combined with soft patterns, they create soothing, restful schemes. Subtle shades contain plenty of white, and therefore work well with white accessories, whether it be in a bathroom, bedroom or lounge. Choose pale furniture – white, colourwashed or light woods, and avoid heavy styles if you can.

Colourwashed walls, with one shade of yellow (or blue) painted roughly over another, are the most forgiving of all wall treatments. This paint technique masks all kinds of rough patches and softens the feel of a room with plain hard lines. Blue on top of yellow, or yellow over blue will give a greenish effect, so its best to stick to different tones of the same colour. Broken colour effects have more depth and luminosity and work in a greater variety of light conditions than solid blocks of colour.

Dark indigo walls lend a grandeur to this bathroom, with the brass fittings echoing the yellow of the starry motifs. Indigo blues suggest luxury, and should be used with confidence.

Primrose yellow and soft blue-grey are partnered in this roughly scumbled bedroom. The effect is reminiscent of a classic country house scheme, while being soft and welcoming. Crisp white bedding accentuates the subtlety of the decor.

Choosing a pattern of blues and yellows which are close in tone will exacerbate the blending effect, making the pattern appear less busy. The careful choice of colour has made this coordinated bathroom scheme appear gentle and restful.

BLUE-GREEN ACCENTS

Turquoise is the sunniest and happiest of blues, and when combined with sunflower yellow makes for a delicious scheme. But this particular blue is at its best when seen alongside cool yellows *and* deeper Prussian blues, as turquoise has the effect of unifying the two. Textile designers often combine the three colours on their fabrics, using either deep blue or turquoise as the accent.

The slightly greyish shades of softer turquoise colours have a cool, silvery quality, while duck egg blues and grey blues go well with cool, muted yellows.

Greeny additions to your blues will add a new dimension to a room scheme. Azure, jade and pale verdigris blues enable you to add metallic yellows such as brass, gold and gilt, both in printed fabrics and accessories.

▶ *Dark blue, cobalt and turquoise are set within this pale blue dining room, contrasted with a creamy yellow – the colour of sand. This same muted yellow tone is picked up in the pale pine table and rush-seated chairs. Blue glass in the lamp and at the window echo the accents on the bold print curtains.*

◀ *This beamed cottage has been given a contemporary look through the use of colour, while losing none of its character. The turquoise sofa provides solid colour, while pale blue and yellow are tied in to the scheme using fabric.*

▲ *Big bold cheques are a perfect choice for this window scheme. The matching cushion and curtain fabric are coordinated with a row of pretty patterned cushions – the colours pulling the whole look together.*

CARIBBEAN COLOURS

Under the tropical sun, tempered by blue sea and sky and lush vegetation, the colour schemes of the Caribbean play at contrasts and harmonies with their vibrant surroundings.

In settings of outstanding natural beauty, where abundant light intensifies every colour, and sizzling temperatures beat man-made colours into muted submission, the accent is on keeping cool. Refreshing white, splashes of sugar-candy pastels and earthy brights colour buildings inside and out, reflecting an indoor-outdoor lifestyle where nature's own bold, tropical colours provide the backdrop.

The Caribbean colour palette is essentially rustic in its simplicity, and retains a mixed heritage of native Indian, African and Colonial influences. Many colour combinations seem delightfully imaginative, bright and spontaneous, just like that essential feature of Caribbean life – Carnival – and all are highlighted by their special, sunshine setting. You can transfer this magic to colder climes – warm up a cool white with a hint of pink, or tone down the glare of a hot sunshine yellow or vibrant blue with a dash of white or grey. By making tonal changes in this way to suit a different kind of light, you can capture the character of the colours without losing their essential vitality.

The unforgettable colours of the Caribbean (above) find their way into an urban interior (above, top), to flood it with warmth and vitality. Toned down to flatter cooler, northern light, the vivid blue, aqua and yellow of the sea and sunshine palette inspire a flattering, contrast colour scheme.

NATURE'S CARIBBEAN COLOURS

When you look at enticing pictures of the Caribbean islands – Trinidad, Tobago, Jamaica, Antigua, the Caymans, to name but a few – glorious images of palm-fringed beaches, jewel-bright sea and sky and dense, tropical vegetation strike you immediately. You can take this lush topography as a basis for a colour scheme, noting how the colours and proportions of earth, sea and sky are balanced. For example, the wonderful colour contrasts of the shoreline, with their subtle variations of tone – the whitened yellows and softened greys of the sands, palest aquas to cobalt blue of the sea and sky, and the muted greens of palms, leave an indelible impression – and a useful term of reference.

So many colours of the Caribbean are vivid, from the fabulous, colour-splash flowers – hibiscus, bougainvillea and orchids – in every bright tint, to the jewel-bright hummingbirds that dart amongst them. Seen in terms of accent colours they are an inspiration – in a lush green or deep blue scheme, for example. The underwater world of the coral reefs is an even more fantastic source of colour and pattern ideas.

In surroundings where nature outdoes even the most flamboyant man-made colour scheme, bright pink woodwork seems almost low key. Transferred from a tropical harbour setting (right) to an apartment interior (above), the pink door strikes a fine balance with the surrounding blues and greens – just as the pretty painted building in the picture does.

In a tropical setting, these rough-cast walls (far left) take a colour lead from their sun and sea setting, to blend gracefully with their surroundings. In an interior thousands of miles away (left), the same colour format creates a calm yet glowing scheme.

The tonal harmony between the sugared almond pinks, mauves and soft creams shown here is typical of the Caribbean palette. Whether in a row of little cottages (below), balanced by the deeper, roof colours, or in a well-proportioned room (right), flattered by the golden tones of the wooden floor and furniture, the effect is delicate and serene.

CARIBBEAN COLOUR SCHEMES

Rough-cast plaster and weathered, sun-baked wood provide the perfect surfaces for a Caribbean colour scheme. On the islands, Colonial influences are seen in bright pastel tints and in the curvy lines of the grander buildings, where the stucco embellishments, highlighted in contrast white against bright yellow ochre, pink, powder blue or grey, have a delightful, almost iced-cake look.

Elsewhere, little wooden houses display a patchwork of coloured detailing under their familiar rust-red, corrugated iron roofs. A distinctive feature is the decorative fretwork trims which adorn the eaves and gables. These are usually painted in hot, sugar-candy colours to match balustrades, doors or window frames, while the wooden plank walls contrast in palm green, yellow or red ochre and shades of turquoise. The overall effects have a refreshingly spontaneous look, and both contrast and blend with their lush surroundings.

Used in a typically Caribbean way to highlight architectural details, these mauves, coral pinks, and aqua greens lift the spirits with their lighthearted quality. This infectious joie de vivre is easily translated in the kitchen shown here, where it brings a spark of individuality to the scheme.

Using the colours

To recreate something of the simple Caribbean style, add plenty of white to make bold pastel tints – in a matt or satin sheen finish – for colourwashed walls and wooden panelling. A bathroom or kitchen is an ideal setting for a rustic Caribbean theme, where you could use contrast colours for decorative medium density fibreboard mouldings and shelving trims along panels, skirtings, picture rails or shelves. Contrast shutters, doors or other wooden details would also reinforce the theme. In larger areas such as a bedroom or living room, you could take soft Caribbean colour harmonies or gentle contrasts and use them as colour blocks. In similar tones, two or three pastel colours on adjacent walls or for furnishings will sit comfortably side by side – balanced with soft whites, natural leafy greens or neutrals.

▶ *Bolder Caribbean contrasts don't necessarily need strong sunlight to balance their impact. In a room with high ceilings and unfussy styling, the contrasts between rich red and yellow have plenty of space to interact without being overpowering.*

◀ *Soft violet blues, used to frame a cool, chalky Caribbean pink, create an understated sense of colour flow from room to room. As with the dark blue shutters in the island house below, the dark sofa helps to create a good tonal balance.*

CARIBBEAN ACCENTS

The essentially happy mood inspired by the sun-bright Caribbean palette can be a useful tool when you want to give an instant boost to a tired scheme. You may not want to create a rustic look, or go for the bolder tropical colour combinations, but in neutral schemes particularly, some strong, toning pastels can make all the difference between a static look or a subtle yet vital scheme.

The energizing qualities of sunshine yellows are well known and, however pale, can add a welcome colour splash. Choose from the warm, buttery yellows or the sharper, citrus tints for accessories and details, and see how well they look with gentle contrasts of aqua and blue. Another trick is to use the natural greens – foliage greens are often surprisingly muted – as a neutral balance or foil for lighter brights.

When you choose the stronger colours as accents, such as the marvellously rich, fuchsia pinks, turquoise and earthy ochres, it helps to create a visual balance by placing two or three of them together. Pictures, fabric prints, lampshades and cushions are all useful tools for this approach.

The tropical colours in the eye-catching picture are a reference point for the group of accessories on the table. Combining accent colours – either in a small group, as here, or to interact with larger areas of plain, bright colour – helps to establish a well-balanced scheme.

With the sky blue wall and deep marine blue accessories, this arrangement conveys the airy relaxed atmosphere of the Caribbean with a minimum of fuss. The vibrant yellow used on the shelf and plant pots make a lively contrast.

GREEN SCHEMES

As nature's splendid neutral, every possible green, from the delicate tints of springtime to the rich and resonant forest shades, has the potential to bring vitality and subtlety to your colour schemes.

The wonderful variety of greens to choose from means that, used carefully, they can flatter almost any room. You can rely on green as the mood takes you, to bring a refreshing touch of the countryside to a scheme, brighten a dull room, create a cool and tranquil setting, or enhance sophisticated styling.

Green is a secondary colour, placed midway on the colour wheel between warm yellow and cool blue – a position that means it also forms a natural balance with complementary red. As they move round the colour wheel, greens vary from the warm lime greens closest to yellow, through the verdant grass greens and cool aqua greens, to the deep forest shades and dark blue-greens. In nature, these harmonies work together beautifully, and this is something you can draw on for your schemes. You can use yellow to draw warmth from an apple green scheme, or you can use clear blue to enhance a blue-green scheme. As a receding colour, green also creates a spacious effect, and this is an advantage in any size room.

Diluted with white, greens provide an easy-on-the-eye background, and a foil for brighter colour accents. Muted with grey – the shades of rosemary, sage and verdigris – greens look subtle and sophisticated; darkened with black, they take on dramatic overtones. As green represents the living colour of nature, it always looks at ease in a scheme with natural materials. Team it with rustic or polished woods, wicker, coir and cotton, silk and wool fabrics and, at its deepest and most sumptuous, with glowing metallic accents.

Springtime Greens

These are the fresh young greens of tender shoots, the acidic greens of lettuce hearts and the juicy, vibrant greens of tropical limes. As a group, springtime greens are at the yellow end of the spectrum, and look bright and sunny, even when diluted with white.

Use these greens as a zesty addition to schemes based on stronger greens, or flatter them with neutrals cream, white and soft grey. Springtime greens complement contrasting coral and fuchsia pink, and create a stimulating counterbalance with cool lilac, lavender and mauve. These colour blends look good as pastels, either worked in traditional, period-style schemes, or for strong and bright contemporary styles.

Looking refreshingly pale and bright, like the first, fragile greens of springtime, the greens in this bathroom are enhanced by clear, crisp white and pretty pattern detailing. The dragged paint effect on the woodwork accentuates the delicate colouring, and a fresh green fern highlights the subtlety of the scheme.

Lettuce-heart green, teamed with neutral, creamy white and delicate pastel blue, looks vibrant and modern in this low-key setting. A clever touch, to balance the impact of so much green, is provided by the muted red and white stripes of the window blind.

▶ Used as an
energizing background
colour, grass greens have a
particular empathy with
warm wood tones, and with
flattering soft whites,
which enhance their cooler
qualities. A scheme based
on these well-balanced,
mid-greens, will harmonize
easily with a blend of
different green tones chosen
for accents and accessories.

▼ Deep and lush, this grass green
colour scheme has an almost
tropical quality. Teamed with vibrant
yellow and complementary blue, the
effect is eye-catching and full of vitality.

Grass Greens

Grass greens are the mid-greens, balanced between yellow and blue, and closest to the true green of the colour wheel. Whether you use them in their deepest tones, or soften them with white, grass greens quietly energize a room. Blend them as accents in schemes based on pale citrus tints, and with contrast rosy pink, cool creamy whites, and to flatter pale-toned and dark wood furniture.

You can create an evocative, summery mood by teaming grass greens with clear white in a simple, uncluttered scheme – either as a mid-tone colour for walls, or as accent details. Emphasize the look with bright green and white stripes or checks, and with foliage plants and ferns. Grass greens work well as one-colour prints with neutrals, and in florals where their strength lends support to a bright colour palette. As pastel tints, these greens look especially pretty with other soft, sugar almond tints.

Aqua Greens

Cool and calming aqua greens are in their watery element in bathrooms and kitchens, and create a restful mood in bedrooms and quiet living areas. These greens have a lot of blue in their make-up, and vary from pale aquamarine tints, through turquoise greens to deepest sea green.

They work especially well as harmonies, used together in a scheme – as in nature – in a range of light to dark aqua green, and with soft, warm-toned neutrals. Pale blues and minty greens flatter the more delicate aquas, as do light woods such as limed pine, beech and birch. Deeper aqua tones look modern and exciting teamed with stronger green accents, especially grass green, olive green and greyed, mustard green. Raspberry pink and soft orange are natural complementaries for aqua green, and work together well as brilliant colour splashes in a vanilla white scheme.

Muted to seaspray green, cool aqua is perfectly balanced by warm wood tones. The calm and orderly effect created by these colours is enhanced by the streamlined styling – perfect for a practical, modern kitchen.

The effect is dramatic, but the mood is tranquil. A range of deep, cool aquas is complemented by sizzling mustard yellow and touches of accent red. The dark lines of the iron furniture and white comforter provide potent highlights.

Deep Greens

As a group, deep greens include clear, bright bottle greens, rich jade greens and the dark and intense forest greens. Strong and vibrant, they look their best in rooms with lots of natural light, where their subtle tones and dramatic potential can be seen to effect, and where dark shadows – which can make these greens look black – are minimized.

Deep ivy greens and dark fir greens have a richness and sophistication that suits formal, period-style schemes. They are a traditional choice in rooms with classic proportions, where high ceilings, large windows and decorative mouldings in a contrast colour can provide a flattering balance. Here you can team them with gleaming metallic accents – mirror and picture frames, and with light-reflecting crystalware and mirrors. Use deep greens wherever you want to create a dramatic, yet warm and intimate atmosphere – in a hall, or in a bathroom, teamed with sparkling white fittings and chrome or warm gold accessories.

Temper the density of these greens with colour contrasts such as glowing terracotta, or with coral or warm violet accents; and with glowing dark wood such as mahogany or, for a low-key look, limed pine or cooled, grey-green wood tones.

Forest green and dark mahogany brown have a rich, masculine feel. Yellow notes in the green tiles are highlighted by spring green drapes and sunny yellow pattern accents.

Illusions – rather than delusions – of grandeur, and a strong sense of humour are indulged in this dramatic hallway. Faux marble effects and classic mouldings are enhanced by deep, rich green – a classic colour choice for sophisticated schemes.

Green Details

You can often use a touch of green to pull a scheme or a look together. Your colour scheme may have no obvious links with green, but, as nature's neutral, a few green details can balance and fine tune a room, especially if something intangible seems to be missing. As house plants and foliage give you a wide variety of green tones, these offer the quickest and easiest way to introduce green accents. You can position larger, floorstanding specimens prominently, or use smaller varieties – topiaries and trailing species – for their shapes, and to create a lively sense of movement.

In a neutral scheme, green details such as piping on cream slip-over chair covers, cushions, or the detailing on a window blind or lampshade, can also add the subtle but refreshing notes necessary to bring a scheme to life.

A warm mid-green, stippled over yellow, provides a vibrant background for mellow wood furniture in a period-style home. The light-enhancing qualities of this colouring are emphasized by the contrast terracotta lampshade and a brilliant pool of light.

Cool aqua tones have a richness that is intensified by strong contrast pinks. Gold metallic accents provide a neutral balancing act between the colours, and would provide a visual bridge with other soft, warm shades in a scheme based on neutral colours.

It would be hard to imagine how this pale yellow, cool white and cream scheme could look better with colour accents other than these deep rich greens. Naturally flattering to mellow wood tones, and at perfect harmony with yellow, the effect has an appealing freshness and vitality.

Greens work harmoniously in nature, so take this as a lead for a green scheme. Choosing from the yellow and blue-toned greens will create a lively balance – especially for accent colours in a contrasting or neutral scheme.

ABSTRACT DESIGNS

*Breathe new life into your home decorating with the innovative ideas
and patterns of abstract art and design. Bold blocks of colour, and
stylized, expressive patterns can invigorate even traditional homes.*

Many people are nervous of using abstract designs in their homes, fearing that the bold colours and vigorous patterns are too dominant to live with, or may look uncomfortable alongside more traditional pieces. However, it's actually quite easy to incorporate some of these ideas and patterns into your existing schemes, or use them as a starting point for new schemes, to create an individual and lively effect.

Some abstract patterns hark back to painters such as Picasso, Matisse and Kandinsky, who used a fluid, expressive style to suggest the essence of the subject rather than a graphic representation. Other painters such as Mondrian

The combination of black, white and primary colours is typical of abstract art and design, and makes for a vibrant scheme. The neutral stone colourwash used on the walls allows the designs to take centre stage; broad striped squabs cleverly echo the monochromatic areas in the paintings.

used geometric forms, with simple blocks of pure colour set alongside each other. Circles, dots, zigzags, and repeating stripes have all been used for centuries as decoration, along with organic, natural forms. Modern artists and designers continue the tradition, often using the sharp contrast of black and white for powerful impact.

BUILDING BLOCKS OF COLOUR

The principles adopted by abstract artists can offer exciting inspiration for decorating schemes, creating calm, simple interiors that are free from fussy details, with satisfying sweeps of plain colour. The colours don't have to be dazzling – subtle combinations of pale grey, honey and lilac, for example, or pale neutral shades, work well too. Try half-closing your eyes as you look round the room, to get a sense of the proportions and shapes in the room. Imagine the walls as a canvas against which the furniture and accessories are silhouetted in blocks of colour.

▶ *In a masterly composition of shapes, this room sets a white paper globe against a deep red wall; further into the room, a shade above the table repeats the effect when a red curtain is drawn at night. The honey tones of the jute matting temper the stark effect.*

▲ *Set against a calm, neutral background, vibrant rugs and furnishing fabrics are given the same emphasis as the prints and paintings on the walls. These strong areas of colour create a warm feel in an otherwise cool living space.*

▶ *Painting part of a wall to match the floor creates a surreal effect – the furniture appears to float before your eyes. A pattern of stripes and bubbles on the upper part of the wall playfully reflects the rust and lime of the colour scheme.*

An unusual and colourful lamp echoes the amorphous shapes and primary hues of abstract art works, set against flat planes of colour in less strident tones of mauve and buttermilk. Every item, from the balancing act of orange and purple seen in the flowers and vases to the fluid white lines of the chairs, is carefully planned to add to the overall effect.

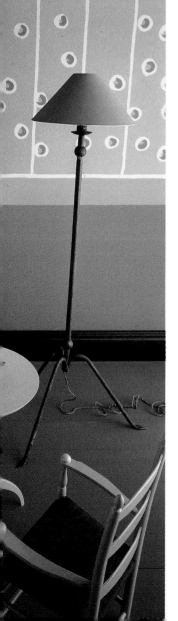

One wall, for example, may present a crisp white background for a chunky deep blue sofa and a modern painting in blues and rusty reds; an adjacent wall may be a rich Chinese red, contrasting with the blue sofa seen from a different part of the room. Add a large lamp with a turquoise shade to cut a triangular cone of colour against the red wall.

By building up blocks of colour in this way, you can give the room a completely new feel. Look at the shape of each piece of furniture carefully; keep the lines as simple as possible and stick to plain colours for the most part so that each piece makes a solid block of colour. Black and white act as highlights, intensifying the other colours around them, or drawing rhythmic lines across pools of colour – for example, the curving arms of a black iron candelabra, or a spherical white lampshade.

The floor area is treated in the same way as the walls: use carpet, floor paint or other coverings such as woodstrip, linoleum or rubber tiles to flood the whole area with a single colour. Against this, geometric rugs and the varied shapes of furniture float in a sea of colour just like a Surrealist painting.

Alternatively, you can introduce the colour block effect on a smaller scale with one or two items that reflect the abstract design influence. Look for paintings and prints that use big flat areas of colour, and hang them above a fireplace or sofa as a focal point. You can also add a large rug, or single-colour throws or cushions, in bright shades. This is an effective way to familiarize yourself with the bolder use of colour involved in the look, and you can create an individualistic living space based on your existing decor.

ABSTRACTED PATTERNS

Another development within the abstract movement used more organic shapes, which were highly stylized and freely drawn – sometimes distorted into strange, dream-like shapes. The influence of artists such as Matisse and Miro is still strong and many fabric designs, ceramic accessories, rugs and other items reflect their style. Look for bold, simplified shapes, which may be outlined in another colour in a loose, painterly style, or overlapping and laid-on shapes. Matisse made a series of paper collages with fluid figures in vivid, exuberant colours. Patterns made up of dots, circles and zigzag lines are almost a visual interpretation of jazz music; scribbled effects or boldly daubed shapes where you can trace the marks of the painter's brush are also typical. Patterns in black and white that almost dance before your eyes are also typical of the look.

Make the most of coordinated ranges inspired by modern art. Here, a jazzy fabric design of scarlet and jade squares splashed on an orange background makes a bold statement, backed up confidently with smaller designs in the wallcovering and cushion fabric.

Soft pretty pastels combined with grey and white make for a restful, calm bedroom. The shapes created by an asymmetric headboard and triangular tables, combined with the vigorously stylized bird design of the duvet cover, give the room a strong modern flavour.

One way of enjoying these expressive, lively designs is to create a blank, empty space similar to an art gallery, allowing the pieces to dominate. Paint all the walls white, and maybe even the floor, although any plain floorcovering will look effective. Then fill the room with as many artistic pieces as you wish, setting colourful rugs, pots, textiles, and pictures one against the other in a kaleidoscope of colour. Visit craft shops, designer accessory shops and art school degree shows to select your own personal collection.

Alternatively, find a bold, confident fabric design and use it in a strong sweep to show off the pattern – as a single floor-to-ceiling curtain, perhaps, or to cover a big sofa. Then echo the colours for the rest of the scheme, maybe incorporating one or two smaller or related patterns, offset with touches of black or white.

◀ *A highly individual collection of colour and pattern makes a bright and welcoming corner. The brilliantly patterned pots, plates, cushions, wall hanging and rug jostle for attention, offering the chance to relax and feast your eyes on each in turn.*

▲ *Designer rugs (above and left) are a wonderful source of colour and pattern; their vibrant tones help define the look of the room. Chosen with care, they make a strong setting for modern furniture and older pieces.*

CREATING YOUR OWN ABSTRACTS

The simple shapes and bold use of colour typical of abstract design make it easy to add your own personal contribution to artistic effort. Update a simple chest or chair with a coat of paint in one colour, then add curving, undulating lines, zigzags or rows of dots down legs or across drawers in a contrasting colour; or paint each drawer of a chest in a different colour. Try your hand with fabric paint on a plain cushion cover – just draw a series of interlocking circles, diamonds or squares, then fill in the shapes they create in different colours. Cut simplified leaf shapes, or strong, stylized bird outlines, from brightly-coloured art paper, and stick them round a contrasting plain lampshade.

Simple, freely drawn diamond motifs appear to float up a wall from a painted band, which creates a line between the offbeat colour scheme of this hallway. Unusual colour mixes need a little confidence – take your inspiration from the teamed colours of modern book jacket designs, wrapping paper or art prints.

These striking, rhythmic lampshade designs show how soothing, neutral colours are brought to life with bold patterns. You can imitate the effect by cutting paper into undulating shapes and setting the shapes a little apart to show narrow strips of the colour beneath.

An uninhibited use of leftover pots of paint gives an old chest witty appeal. The undulating lines of the fascia board on top of the chest have prompted a repeated use of similar wavy lines, and the colours are linked carefully with accessories such as pots and candlesticks.

STIPPLING

*Stippling is one of the most delicate paint finishes,
producing soft freckles of colour that merge together to give
the surface a subtly mottled appearance.*

The finely flecked appearance of stippling makes it an attractive paint finish for all kinds of surfaces – from small accessories, such as lampshades, to large expanses of wall, where it provides a flattering, low-key background for pictures and furnishings.

A stippled effect is achieved by applying a coloured glaze over a paler base coat. You then use a special stippling brush or pad to lift off flecks of the glaze with a "bouncing" action.

The technique is the same whether you use a stippling brush or a stippling pad, but the brush gives a subtler effect. Both are available from home decor and craft stores, and you can also buy the brushes from artists' suppliers. Stippling brushes come in a wide range of sizes – use a large brush for large surface areas, such as walls, and a small brush for accessories.

Water-based paints are easy to work with but dry rapidly, so you need to work quickly. If you plan to stipple a large area, you might prefer to use oil-based paints, which dry more slowly, giving you more time to work the glaze.

➤ *A fine stippled finish adds distinction to a bookcase, and gives it a smart, contemporary look. If you want to stipple on a painted piece of furniture, you don't need to start from scratch. Just clean the surface and stipple on top, using a pale or brightly coloured glaze, depending on the existing base coat colour.*

STIPPLING A SURFACE

Before you start

Traditionally, stippling uses a pale shade for the base coat, with a darker shade for the glaze, but you can reverse this if you wish. Make sure your chosen colours are not too close in tone, or the effect will be lost. You can either use a ready-tinted glaze, or buy a clear glaze and tint it to the desired shade yourself, following the manufacturer's instructions.

Practise the stippling technique on scrap card, using your chosen colours, before you start on the surface.

YOU WILL NEED

- ➤ Emulsion paint for base coat
- ➤ Water-based glaze, ready-tinted or clear
- ➤ Emulsion or artists' acrylic paint for tinting the glaze (optional)
- ➤ Paint roller (optional)
- ➤ Paintbrush
- ➤ Stippling brush or pad
- ➤ Clean rag or paper towel
- ➤ Clear, matt or satin acrylic varnish

FINE STIPPLING USING A BRUSH

1 Make sure the surface is clean and dust free. Use a paint roller or brush to apply an even base coat in the desired colour to the surface. Leave to dry.

2 Tint the glaze to the desired shade, if necessary. Use a paintbrush to apply a thin, even film of glaze to the surface, criss-crossing the brush strokes. Work on a small area at a time – a vertical strip about 60cm (2ft) wide on a wall, for example – as the glaze dries quickly. On a wood surface, apply the glaze in the direction of the grain.

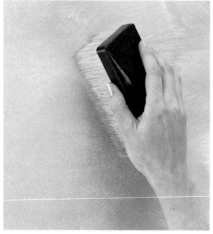

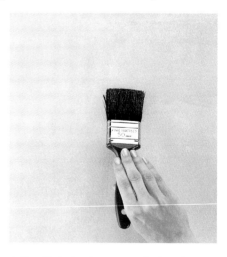

3 If working on an edged surface, such as a shelf or table top, stipple the edge first; otherwise the brush strokes will overlap the top of the surface and disturb the finish. Hold the stippling brush at right angles to the edge and strike the glaze lightly but firmly with the bristles.

4 Stipple the surface as in step 3, "bouncing" the stippling brush across the surface and keeping it at right angles to prevent skidding; vary the direction of the brush to achieve a random effect. Remove any build-up of glaze on the brush at regular intervals by dabbing it on a clean rag or paper towel. Leave the surface to dry thoroughly.

5 If desired, use a paintbrush to apply two coats of matt or satin varnish to the surface, allowing the varnish to dry between coats.

COARSE STIPPLING USING A PAD

Follow **Fine stippling using a brush**, steps 1 and 2. Hold the stippling pad at right angles to the surface, and bounce it across the surface – keep your wrist loose as the stippling pad doesn't have much spring. Once you have stippled the whole glazed area, repeat, using a slightly lighter touch. Remove any build-up of glaze on the pad at regular intervals. Leave to dry. Finish as for **Fine stippling using a brush**, step 5.

Stippling a large surface

If stippling a large area, such as a wall, follow these guidelines:

● Use an oil-based paint and glaze, which stay workable for longer.

● Ask a friend to help you – one of you can apply the glaze while the other stipples the surface. This prevents 'tide marks' forming where one band of glaze has dried before the next has been applied. Complete a whole wall in one session.

● Stand back to check the overall effect at regular intervals. If there are any dark patches, dab the brush lightly at them to lift off some more glaze; if there are light patches, pick up a touch of glaze on the brush bristles and carefully stipple the glaze on to the wall.

● Use a small brush, such as a paintbrush or stencil brush, to stipple in corners.

Colour effects

Experiment with a range of colour combinations to see all the different effects you can achieve with stippling.

Turquoise Apply a pale powder blue base coat, then a stronger Mediterranean blue glaze, and stipple using a stippling brush.

Sage green Apply a pale pistachio base coat, then a sage green glaze, and stipple using a stippling brush.

Yellow Apply a cream-coloured base coat, then a buttercup yellow glaze, and stipple using a stippling brush.

Small accessories, such as these Shaker-style storage boxes, are quick to stipple and show off the delicate finish well. If you are only planning to stipple a small item and don't want to invest in a stippling brush, experiment with alternatives – a clean shoe brush or an old soft-bristle hair brush will do just as well, provided the bristles are all the same length.

A finely stippled wall provides an attractive backdrop for furnishings of any style. Experiment with stippling on a small item or a piece of lining paper before embarking on a wall, as it takes practice to achieve an even effect.

You can stipple home accessories to match your colour scheme. This wooden tray was stippled with dark blue glaze over a light blue base coat, using a stippling brush. The two shades of blue perfectly echo those in the tablecloth fabric.

The plastic bristles of a stippling pad give a far more noticeable, coarse-grained effect than a brush. On this wall, a pad has been used to stipple intense purple glaze over a lilac base coat, creating a rich depth of colour.

GRADED PAINT EFFECTS

*A graded paint effect has soft bands of colour – usually ranging
from light to dark – which drift seamlessly into one another,
creating an effect that is both dramatic and easy on the eye.*

To create a graded paint finish, tinted glazes in different shades are applied in bands over a base coat, and stippled to merge the colours and soften the effect. You can either work the finish in different tones of the same colour – as in the graded blue effect shown here; or you can use a range of colours – this works best if you keep to neighbouring colours on the colour wheel, working from pink, through purple to blue, for example. For the base coat, you can use either plain white, or a pale colour that tones with the tinted glazes.

Use a clear, slow-set water-based glaze, available from artists' suppliers, and tint it to the desired shade using latex paint or artists' acrylics; using a slow-set glaze gives you more time for stippling, and is essential if you are painting a large surface. For the base coat, use satin latex, which gives a smooth, slightly slippery base to work on. If you prefer, you can use slower-drying oil-based paints and glazes instead.

 *This graded paint effect in shades of blue is reminiscent of a hazy summer sky. The finish has been applied above the chair rail only, and is balanced by trimwork painted in mid-blue.*

SINGLE-COLOUR GRADED EFFECT

YOU WILL NEED

- Satin latex in white or other pale colour
- Paint roller and tray
- Slow-set, water-based clear glaze
- Bowl for mixing

- Latex paint in desired colour
- Stick for mixing paint
- Paintbrush
- Stippling brush
- Acrylic varnish (optional)

Before you start

When creating a single-colour graded effect, you always start with the palest tone glaze and finish with the darkest. This is because the same glaze is used throughout – you simply keep adding small amounts of colour to darken the glaze before moving on to the next stage. When creating a multi-coloured graded effect, you need to mix a separate tinted glaze for each colour; you can apply the glazes in the order of your choice.

Although slow-set glaze gives you more working time, you still need to work quickly; if possible, enlist a friend to mix and apply the glaze while you stipple, or vice versa.

1 Make sure the surface is smooth and dust free. Use a paint roller to apply two or three coats of the vinyl silk emulsion, allowing the paint to dry between coats. Leave the surface to dry thoroughly.

2 Pour the slow-set glaze into a bowl – make sure you pour out enough to complete the whole project. Apply a very small amount of the coloured latex paint to the glaze and mix well to create the palest tone of your graded effect.

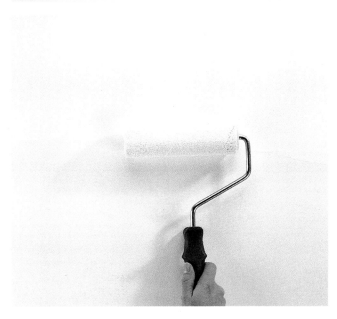

3 Use a paintbrush to apply the tinted glaze to one end of the surface – the end that will be palest in the finished graded effect; apply the glaze thinly and evenly, in broad brush strokes.

4 Use a stippling brush to stipple the glaze, holding it at right angles to the surface and striking the glaze lightly but firmly, in a bouncing motion. Work quickly, from one side of the surface across to the other, changing the angle of your wrist so you stipple in a series of small semi-circles for an even effect. Remove any build-up of glaze on the brush at regular intervals by dabbing it on a clean rag.

5 Apply a little more coloured latex to the glaze, as in step 2, and mix well to give a slightly darker tone – the mid tone of the graded effect. Brush the glaze on to the surface next to the previous glaze, and stipple as before, softly merging the colours where the two glazes meet. Stand back to check the effect at regular intervals, and rectify any uneven patches.

6 Repeat step 5 to mix and apply the darkest tone of glaze, and stipple it as before.

7 Leave the surface to dry thoroughly. If desired, repeat steps 2-6 to intensify the colour and add depth. For a more durable finish, apply two coats of acrylic varnish, allowing the varnish to dry thoroughly between coats.

Colour effects

Green and blue Glazes in pale and medium tones of green lead into a rich bluish purple, creating a fresh colour combination that takes its inspiration from nature.

Purple and pink The purple and pink glazes used to create this effect are neighbours on the colour wheel, making for dramatic but perfectly harmonious results.

Citrus shades Tangy yellow merging into lime green makes for a wonderfully fresh graded finish – a great one to try out in a bathroom, on walls or accessories depending on how brave you feel.

▼ *Glazes in cool turquoise and blue were applied over a sea green base coat to create the glorious range of tones and depth of colour on this wall. The slightly softer, cloudy effect is achieved by using a damp sponge instead of a stippling brush to merge and soften the glazes.*

▲ *A shaped firescreen becomes a rich colour accent when decorated with a graded paint effect in glowing flame shades. Strong colours such as these can be overpowering on walls, but are terrific for brightening up accessories.*

◄ *This storage chest has been given a subtle, one-colour graded finish, using palest yellow through citrus to saffron. If you are decorating an accessory that will undergo a fair amount of wear and tear, it's essential to apply at least two coats of acrylic varnish to protect the finish.*

UPDATING OLD TILES

Treat your kitchen or bathroom to a new, up-to-the-minute look, without the expense and effort of re-tiling, by using special tile primers and finishes to transform the tiles.

If you've recently moved or you haven't decorated for a while, you may find that the tiles in your kitchen or bathroom have started to look old and worn. Or they may simply clash with your new plans and colour schemes for these rooms. As interior trends change, room schemes using browns and beiges, or tiles with dated designs, may start to look old-fashioned in modern kitchens and bathrooms.

Re-tiling can be quite a messy and expensive project, and your budget may not stretch to replacing tiles completely. However, if the tiles are in fairly good condition and it's just the colour or pattern you object to, an easy solution is to give them a facelift rather than replace them. Even if your tiles are cracked or

chipped, they can be patched up and decorated to give them a completely new look.

If you paint over old tiles, it's best to use a special tile paint system. This includes a base cleaner, a primer, colour coating in a choice of shades, and a durable top coat with a satin or gloss finish. In addition, you can buy strips of stick-on grouting in a variety of neutral colours, as well as in red, brown and black if you want to make the grouting into a feature. All these products are available by mail order and from some home improvement stores.

When you have painted the tiles, you can add decorative effects of your choice, using a stencil, stamp or paint finish such as sponging, for example. Apply these before you paint on the protective top coating.

For a lively, three-dimensional look, apply stick-on ceramic motifs randomly over your redecorated tiled surface. There is a variety of designs to choose from, including fish or seashells for a bathroom, or fruit and vegetables for a kitchen. Here, bright red stick-on grouting has also been added to create a cheerful finishing touch.

PAINTING OVER TILES

- ➤ Household bleach and scrubbing brush
- ➤ Masking tape and old newspapers or sheets
- ➤ Fine surface filler
- ➤ Abrasive paper, fine grade
- ➤ Old paintbrush

- ➤ Tile Make-up System – base cleaner, wash primer, colour coating, joint strips and protective coating
- ➤ Small roller with spare rollers and paint tray
- ➤ Clean cloths
- ➤ Rubber gloves

The colour coating is available in a range of neutral colours, including white, light grey, light blue and beige, which will suit a variety of room schemes. If you want a more colourful finish, you can apply a coat of plain acrylic or latex paint in a brighter colour, or finish the tiles with a special decorative effect, such as one of those shown on page 112. However, bear in mind that acrylic and latex paints won't be as durable as special tile paints.

PREPARING THE SURFACE

1 Scrub the tiles using a solution of bleach and water to remove mould. Remove any old silicone mastic from the grouting between the tiles. Fill any cracks or chips by smoothing tile grout or a fine filler over the tiles and joins, taking care to work it into chipped areas. When dry, sand the surface smooth; wipe off dust with a damp cloth.

2 Following the manufacturer's instructions, carefully spray the base cleaner on to the tiles and spread it over the entire surface using a clean cloth. Leave it to dry thoroughly. The base cleaner will remove any remaining grease or dirt from the surface.

Simple guidelines

● To achieve a professional-looking finish, it's essential to keep the work area surrounding the tiles clean and tidy. To ensure that the area remains dirt and dust free, vacuum before you start and between each step, as necessary. If dust sticks to the tiled surface as you apply the colour coating and protective finish, it may spoil the finished effect.

● Protect any areas immediately adjacent to your work surface by masking them off with tape. Use old newspapers or sheets to protect the surrounding area from any splashes or accidental spills.

● Make sure you use old clean cloths to apply the base cleaner and wash primer, and an old paintbrush to apply the colour coating, as they can't be cleaned and you will have to throw them away after use.

3 Spray an even coating of the wash primer over the tiles, then spread it over the entire surface using a clean, soft cloth. Leave it to dry for at least 30 minutes before starting to paint the tiles.

PAINTING AND GROUTING

1 Wearing rubber gloves, use the paintbrush to apply the colour coating to the grouted areas; paint an area of about 1m (1yd) square at a time. Using the roller, apply an even layer of colour coating before the brushed-on paint dries. Repeat to cover the entire surface; leave to dry for at least six hours. Apply a second coat using the roller only; leave to dry for at least 12 hours.

2 When the paint has dried completely to form a hard finish, lightly sand the surface using fine-grade abrasive paper. Do not worry if you remove the gloss from the painted surface, as the protective covering applied in step 4 provides the satin or gloss finish required. Brush off the dust and vacuum the area before continuing.

3 If you wish to add coloured grouting, measure the full length of both the horizontal and vertical grouted areas between the tiles. Cut enough strips of stick-on grouting to these measurements, adding an extra 3cm (1¼in) to each strip. Peel off a little of the paper backing and stick each strip on to the old grouted areas; press the strips with your finger and remove the backing as you go. Apply the horizontal strips first, followed by the vertical ones, pressing down firmly where the two meet. Smooth over the strips with a damp cloth to secure the edges.

4 Using a clean roller, apply the protective coating in either a satin or gloss finish, as desired. Leave to dry for at least 24 hours before allowing the tiles to come into contact with water. If a more hardwearing finish is required, apply extra layers of the protective coating.

➤ *If you wish to add a decorative painted finish to your revamped tiles, apply your chosen design before step 4, leaving the paint to dry completely before adding the protective coating. This simple flower motif is easy to stencil on to the prepared tile surface – just a few, placed here and there, are ideal for breaking up the monotony of a plain tiled surface.*

DECORATIVE DESIGN IDEAS

When you have finished painting your tiles, you might like to add a decorative finish, such as a stencil, special paint effect or stick-on motifs. To ensure a permanent finish, add any design details before you apply the protective coating – except for stick-on motifs, which are applied after the protective coating.

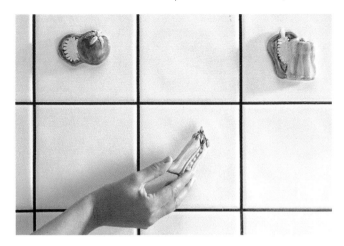

Stick-on motifs are easy to apply and give an instant new look to a plain tiled surface. There is a wide range of designs to choose from. To add the motifs, you simply peel off the paper backing and stick them in place.

Sponging creates an attractive mottled effect all over the tiled surface. You can simply sponge one colour over a plain or coloured base colour, or sponge two colours in contrasting or complementary tones, depending on the effect required.

Freehand designs add a charming handpainted finish to tiles. You can paint a pattern all over the surface, or just decorate a few individual tiles. Abstract designs, such as stripes or swirls, work well. To achieve the dotted effect above, simply twizzle a stencil brush on to the tiled surface.

Stencilling gives a neat, professional finish and re-creates the effect of patterned tiles. You can build up layers of colour to give subtle, shaded effects. For the best results, use a special tile stencil, like the one shown above, or you can adapt a small motif from a standard stencil.

Stamping is a quick and easy alternative to stencilling. There's an amazing range of stamps to choose from so simply select one to suit your room. This starfish design is perfect for a bathroom with a seaside theme.

WOODEN SHELF TRIMS

Add interest to a plain shelf kit by using wooden fretwork trims. They come in a variety of designs, from simple curves to intricate lacework, and create an eye-catching effect which is easy to achieve.

Edge trim is a border strip made from plywood or medium density fibreboard (MDF) which has a machine-cut, ornamental profile. The trim comes in a range of designs to complement any style of interior – from soft scallops and rolling waves to sharp geometric shapes and delicate pierced patterns.

Sold in specialist home improvement stores and by mail order, edge trim is inexpensive and very simple to work, requiring the minimum of woodworking skills. It comes in a variety of depths and in 1220mm (48in) lengths, which you can cut to size with a fine-toothed tenon saw. If you require a longer run, the lengths are designed to butt together without interrupting the flow of the pattern.

To fix the trim on to a shelf, or any other flat wooden surface, you can

These scallop-trimmed shelves make a colourful addition – and create useful storage space. The trim has been added to plain kit-form shelves, then painted before being fixed to the wall.

use either woodworking adhesive and panel pins, or a hot glue gun. Once in place, you can paint the trim to match or contrast with the shelf.

MAKING TRIMMED SHELVES

Shelf kits, complete with brackets and fixings, are perfect candidates for edge trims. You can fix the trim so the decorative edge points down, as here, or up. If the shelf has a bevelled edge, place this towards the wall and fix the trim along the straight edge. Alternatively, add the trim to an existing shelf.

How much trim?
To work out how much edge trim you need, measure the shelf length then add the length of two edge trim pattern repeats.

YOU WILL NEED

- Wooden shelf kit
- Edge trim
- Set square and pencil
- Tenon saw
- Medium and fine grade abrasive paper
- Wood adhesive
- Panel pins, 2cm (¾in)
- Pin hammer

- Nail punch
- Wood filler
- Decorating brush
- Wood primer and paint
- Level
- Tape measure
- Screwdriver
- Bradawl
- Power drill and masonry bit

ADDING THE TRIM

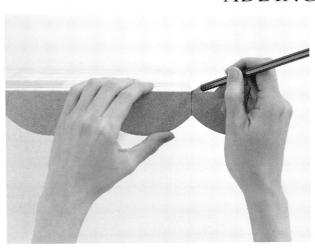

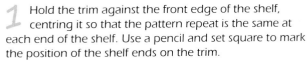

1 Hold the trim against the front edge of the shelf, centring it so that the pattern repeat is the same at each end of the shelf. Use a pencil and set square to mark the position of the shelf ends on the trim.

2 Cut the trim at the marks using a tenon saw, then sand the ends smooth with medium grade abrasive paper. Apply wood adhesive to the front edge of the shelf and stick the trim in place.

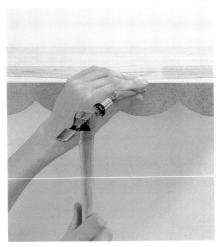

3 While the adhesive is still wet, hammer in panel pins to secure the trim. Position one close to each end, one in the centre and space the rest about 10cm (4in) apart. Wipe off any excess adhesive.

4 Drive the pin heads below the surface of the trim using a narrow nail punch, then fill the holes with wood filler. Allow this to dry then sand it smooth with fine grade abrasive paper.

5 Apply a coat of wood primer to a bare wood shelf and brackets or use abrasive paper to sand down a shelf and brackets that are already painted. Apply undercoat then two coats of top coat, allowing each coat to dry before sanding lightly and applying the next coat.

TIP

Cupboard shelves

If you are adding edge trim to existing shelves inside a cupboard, check that the doors will close before you fix the trim in place. You may need to trim off the front or back edge of the shelves to allow for the extra thickness.

▶ *For speedy results, use a hot glue gun to stick the trim in place. Apply glue along the shelf's front edge, following the manufacturer's instructions. There's no need to secure with panel pins.*

PUTTING UP THE SHELF

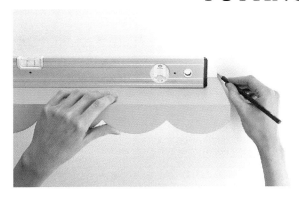

1 Hold the shelf in position, placing a level on top to make sure the shelf is level. On the wall, mark a point at each end of the shelf and a guideline along the lower edge of the shelf. Measure the shelf length and divide by four, then mark the bracket positions this distance in from each end of the shelf guideline.

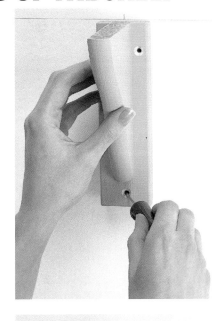

2 If necessary, assemble the brackets following the kit instructions. Hold one bracket in position, aligning the top edge with the guideline. Mark the screw hole positions with a bradawl. Using a drill and masonry bit, drill 2.5cm (1in) holes at the marks. Insert the wall plugs provided and screw the bracket in place.

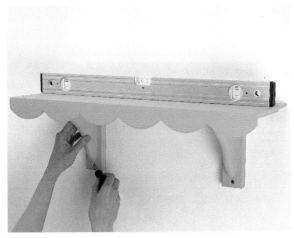

3 Hold the other bracket in position and rest the shelf on top. Place a level on the shelf and adjust the bracket until the shelf is level. Mark and fix the bracket to the wall as before.

4 Centre the shelf on the brackets and secure it to each bracket with a panel pin. Touch up the paintwork to conceal the screw and pin heads. If desired, seal the shelf with a coat of clear polyurethane varnish.

A wave trim adds a nautical touch to this bathroom shelf. You can even use the crests of the "waves" to hang small towels.

A collection of ornaments, all in a floral theme, are perfectly complemented by this stylized fleur-de-lys edge trim. To highlight the display, you could conceal a narrow strip light behind the overhanging trim.

A delicate fretwork trim adds a feminine touch to these recessed bedroom shelves. To reinforce the lacy effect, the shelves are painted a soft shade of milky white.

FAUX STAINED GLASS

*Re-create the glowing colours and eye-catching patterns
of stained glass on a plain window, using glass paints and self-
adhesive lead strip. The results are realistic and longlasting.*

Stained glass windows are an asset in any home, drawing the eye and setting the room aglow with colour. With the right materials, you can mimic stained glass with very convincing results. You simply paint on the design using special glass paints, then outline the painted sections with self-adhesive lead strip.

Glass paints are available from art and craft shops and mail order suppliers in a wide range of colours, which you can mix to create an even broader palette. Once dry they are washable with soapy water, but won't withstand scrubbing and harsh detergents. You can buy lead strip from craft stores in a range of widths. To use it, you cut it to the desired length and smooth it in place on the glass, removing the peel-off backing as you go. You then use a

▲ *A faux stained glass design in bright jewel colours transforms this plain square window into a focal point. Simple, geometric designs like this, with just a few straight lines, are ideal for a beginner.*

boning tool (available with the lead strip) to secure it firmly in place. Precise instructions vary for both the glass paints and the lead strip, so it's important to follow the manufacturer's recommendations closely.

You can use any design you like for your window, but bear in mind the scale and shape. It's best to keep to a fairly simple design with straight lines rather than curves if this is your first attempt.

CREATING A FAUX STAINED GLASS WINDOW

Before you start

Clean the window thoroughly to remove dirt and grease, then wipe over it with a clean, dry cloth. If you are mixing glass paints to achieve the colour you desire, make sure you mix up enough to complete the project – it is difficult to match a colour exactly second time round. Read through the manufacturer's instructions for your glass paints and self-adhesive lead strip before you begin, and follow them carefully.

YOU WILL NEED

- ➤ Steel tape measure
- ➤ Pencil, ruler and set square
- ➤ Large piece of paper
- ➤ Scissors
- ➤ Masking tape
- ➤ Artists' paintbrush
- ➤ Glass paints in desired colours
- ➤ Self-adhesive lead strip
- ➤ Boning tool

1 Measure the width and height of your window, inside the window frame. Use a pencil, ruler and set square to draw a square or rectangle to this size on paper, and cut it out. For an arched or round window, lay a large piece of paper over the window, and crease it firmly along the edges of the glass; cut along the crease lines and check the fit. Mark out your stained glass design on the paper template.

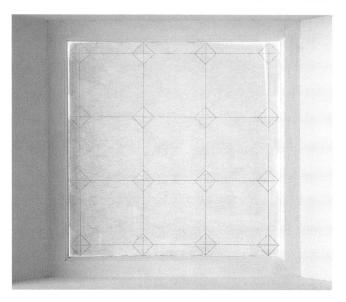

2 Use masking tape to stick your design on to the back of the window, so that you can see it through the glass from the right side. Stand back and check the effect – make sure that the design looks balanced and is a suitable scale for the window. Make adjustments if necessary.

3 Using an artists' brush, apply the first glass paint colour to the window, carefully following the design lines on your drawing; load the brush generously, but not so much that the paint will drip or run on the surface. Work quickly, blending the brush strokes to keep the colour as even as possible. Complete all the areas in that colour.

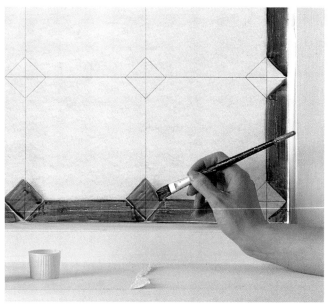

4 When the first paint colour is dry, start applying the next colour, keeping within the design outlines as before, and taking care not to allow the paint to travel into adjacent colour areas.

5 When the second paint colour is dry, move on to the next colour. Continue applying the paints, one colour at a time, until the design is complete. If you wish, when the paints are completely dry, you can apply a second coat to deepen and intensify the colour. Leave to dry thoroughly.

6 Cut a piece of self-adhesive lead strip to the required length for one of the design lines – start with the longest lines. Smooth out the lead strip with your finger. Peel away the backing paper from one end of the strip, and position it on the window. Use finger pressure to smooth the strip in place, peeling away the backing paper as you go. Use the boning tool to secure the strip firmly in place, first along the lead surface, then along each edge. Repeat to apply lead strip to the other main design lines.

7 Repeat step 6 to apply lead strip to the shorter design lines, until the design is complete. Where lead strips meet, avoid butt-joining the ends; either overlap them and press them firmly in place, or, wherever possible, tuck loose ends under a solid lead strip.

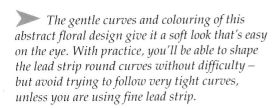

▶ *The gentle curves and colouring of this abstract floral design give it a soft look that's easy on the eye. With practice, you'll be able to shape the lead strip round curves without difficulty – but avoid trying to follow very tight curves, unless you are using fine lead strip.*

DESIGN IDEAS

When deciding on a design for your window, make sure it suits your room scheme in both colour and style; it should also be in proportion to the size of the window, and flatter its shape. It's a good idea to make a few scaled-down drawings of your window, then mark on and colour in some different design options – the one you finally choose can serve as a useful colour reference when you come to paint the window.

Here are three designs – for a square, a rectangular and an arched window – which you can enlarge and use if you wish.

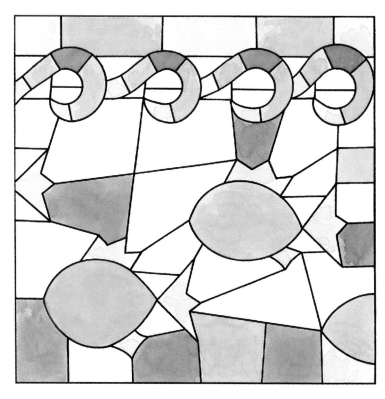

▶ *This fun, light-hearted design of fish and waves in aquas, blues and yellow is ideal for a square bathroom window – what better way to brighten up bathtime?*

◀ *This autumnal scene of a tree shedding its leaves is a good choice for a rectangular window in a traditional room scheme. The golds, greens and browns used to paint the glass make an elegantly understated colour combination.*

▶ *Crisp and contemporary, this geometric design takes its inspiration from all things nautical. Its combination of curves and straight lines is the perfect foil for an arched window.*

TESSERAE MOSAIC

*Mini glass tiles, known as tesserae, arranged into
a mosaic design can be used to customize plain table
tops, trays and other pieces of furniture.*

Mosaic designs complement modern interiors beautifully and they have become a popular choice for decorating home accessories. You can use all sorts of items – from pieces of broken crockery to shells and pebbles – to form mosaic patterns. But if you want to create a smooth surface and regular effect, opt instead for tesserae.

Machine-cut tesserae tiles, approximately 2cm (¾in) square, are easy to work with and are available in a breathtaking range of colours from some art and craft shops and specialist tile suppliers. You can buy tiles all in one colour by the square foot, either loose or attached to a paper backing sheet, or as a mixed bag containing a variety of colours. Prices vary depending on colour, with more unusual colours costing the most.

You can add tesserae to any item that is strong, well-made and has a fairly flat surface. Use them in a bathroom or kitchen, interspersed between conventional tiles. Or cover the whole surface, say of a picture or mirror frame. As the surface of the tiles is smooth and waterproof, they are perfect for decorating table tops, splashbacks and window ledges.

Because of their shape and size, tesserae tiles are the perfect choice for creating even lines, borders and for outlining shapes. Use them to create a striking geometric design or chequerboard effect, for example.

DECORATING A TABLE TOP

Before you start

Tesserae tiles can make items surprisingly heavy, so bear this in mind when choosing an item you'd like to cover with mosaic. If you are using the tiles for a splashback, or if you want to use the item outdoors, use waterproof adhesive and grout to fix the tiles in place.

YOU WILL NEED

- ➤ Tape measure
- ➤ Paper, plain or squared
- ➤ Coloured pencils
- ➤ Pencil
- ➤ Craft knife
- ➤ PVA adhesive (optional)

- ➤ Straightedge or templates (optional)
- ➤ Tesserae tiles
- ➤ Tile nippers and safety goggles
- ➤ Rubber gloves
- ➤ Tile adhesive

- ➤ Adhesive spreader or old knife
- ➤ Tile grout
- ➤ Artists' acrylic paint (optional)
- ➤ Grout spreader
- ➤ Sponge

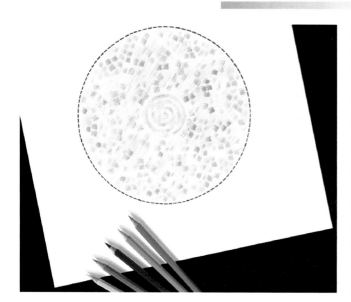

1 Make a scale drawing of the surface or area to be decorated. Mark the mosaic design on the drawing, using coloured pencils to represent the different colour areas. For a geometric design you can use squared paper and mark out the design with one square on the paper representing one mosaic tile.

2 Use a pencil to mark the outlines of the mosaic design on the surface being decorated, using your scale drawing as a guide. Depending on your mosaic design, mark the outlines freehand or use a straightedge or make templates to draw round.

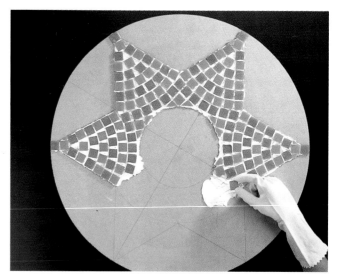

3 Thoroughly clean the surface you are tiling. If it is made of wood, use a craft knife to score the surface diagonally to the grain for better adhesion. Seal an absorbent surface, such as wood, plaster or terracotta, with PVA adhesive.

4 Wearing rubber gloves, apply tile adhesive about 3mm (1/8in) thick, to a section of one main colour area, using an adhesive spreader or palette knife. Keep the design outlines visible. Press the tiles, grooved side down, into the adhesive, spaced about 3mm (1/8in) apart. Cover each main colour area in this way, wiping off excess adhesive from the surface as you work. The adhesive takes about 20 minutes to set, so you can reposition tiles if needed.

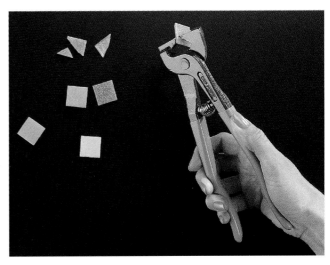

5 Fill in the detail areas of the design, applying tile adhesive to the grooved side of each tile then pressing it firmly into place. If desired, cut the tiles to shape following step 6.

6 If you want to cut shapes or fill in spaces, use tile nippers or pincers to clip the tiles to the shape required. Wear safety goggles to protect your eyes from glass splinters. Insert the tile in the nippers, aligning the blade with the required cut. Squeeze the handles of the nippers together. To apply more pressure, hold the nippers near the end of the handles.

7 Continue to cover the surface with tiles following your design outlines. If necessary, tile the edges or rim of the surface, applying the adhesive to the surface or back of the tile as preferred. Leave to dry for 24 hours.

8 Using a grout spreader, apply a thick layer of grout over the tesserae, pushing it into the gaps. If desired use a coloured grout or mix artists' acrylic paint into the grout to colour it.

9 Wipe off any excess grout with a damp sponge. Check the grout is even, and press a little more into the gaps between the tiles if necessary. Leave the grout to dry, then wipe over the surface again with a clean damp sponge to give it a shine.

Small ceramic tiles can be used in the same way as glass tesserae tiles to create interesting mosaic effects. Here, a shallow terracotta dish has been covered inside and out with tiles, then filled with water to make an attractive miniature water garden.

Make an up-to-the-minute statement with a tesserae tile splashback in shades of cool blue and turquoise. Toning accessories – the mirror frame, handtowel and toiletries bag – echo the splashback colours.

Tesserae tiles make a perfect edging for conventional ceramic tiles. In this bathroom a border of coloured tesserae tiles has been used to add definition to a plain white ceramic tile splashback, and as a decorative edging on the bathroom shelf.

Customize a mirror frame with tesserae tiles. Simple but effective designs are easy to create – here a chequerboard outer border in bronze and silvery grey tiles frames inner borders in mixed shades of grey.

PAINTED CUSHIONS

*Use fabric paints and pens, and simple paint techniques
such as stamping and sponging to transform plain
cushions into unique home accessories.*

Fabric paints and pens come in a wide range of colours and finishes, from bright glossy primaries to dimensional "puff" paints and eye-catching metallics. You can use them to create a dazzling range of looks on plain cushion covers – either by painting freehand, or by using basic painting tools such as stamps and stencils.

Fabric paints tend to work best on natural fabrics with a fairly smooth finish – cotton, linen or silk cushion covers are

ideal. Slip a piece of thick card into the cushion before you begin painting, to give a firm working surface and to stop the paint seeping through to the back.

As an inexpensive and fun alternative to shop-bought stencils and stamps, you can use ordinary household materials as pattern-makers and templates. Rough parcel string stuck to a small block of wood makes an effective stamp, for example, and you can use masking tape to create strong geometric designs.

Classic looks A pair of cushions in vibrant colours sets off these classical images, which have been applied to the covers using an Image Maker kit – a design transfer tool from craft suppliers. You simply photocopy your chosen image, enlarge or reduce it to the desired size, then follow the manufacturer's instructions to transfer it on to the cushion front.

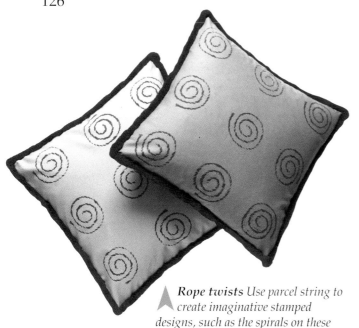

Rope twists Use parcel string to create imaginative stamped designs, such as the spirals on these furry-edged cushions. To make the stamp, glue a piece of string in a spiral shape on to a block of wood. Apply fabric paint to the string with a small paint roller, and stamp the design.

Acid stripes You can use masking tape and fabric paints to create simple but striking geometric designs on plain cushion covers. Firmly press lengths of masking tape on to the cushion front to create irregular stripes – some straight, some on the diagonal; then use a small damp sponge to apply paint to the unmasked areas. Leave to dry, then peel off the tape and set the paints.

Dotty silk Silk cushions in subtle shades have been enlivened with the help of bright pink and gold dots, applied freehand using fabric paints. First use a slim artists' brush and gold paint to draw small circles all over the front of the cushion, using the end of a pencil as a template. When this is dry, apply the dots of bright pink paint.

INDEX

Page numbers in *italic* refer to captions and illustrations

PICTURE ACKNOWLEDGMENTS

Photographs:
7(bl,br) Robert Harding Syndication/IPC/Ideal Home, 8(tl) Robert Harding Syndication/IPC/Homes & Gardens, (tr) Harris, (b) Robert Harding Syndication/IPC/Homes & ideas, 9(t) Boras, (bl) Robert Harding Syndication/Country Homes & Interiors/Polly Wreford, 10(t) Sanderson, (bl) Next Interior, 11(t) IKEA, (br) Eaglemoss/Graham Rae, 12(tr) Do It All, 12-13 Robert Harding Syndication/Ideal Home/Dominic Blackmore, 14(tr) Elizabeth Whiting & Associates/Brian Harrison, (bl) Elizabeth Whiting & Associates/Michael Dunne, 15(tc) Eaglemoss/Graham Rae, (tr) Elizabeth Whiting & Associates/Tom Leighton, (br) Do It All, 16(tr) Do It All, (cl) Robert Harding Syndication/Ideal Home/Dominic Blackmore, (bl) Eaglemoss/Graham Rae, (br) Do It All, 17(t) Doehetzelf, (br) Eaglemoss/Steve Tanner, 18(br) Robert Harding Syndication/Homes & Ideas/Andrew Cameron, 19 IKEA, 20(bl) Abode Interiors, (br) Marie Claire Maison, 20-21(tc) Robert Harding Syndication/Homes & Ideas/Dominic Blackmore, 21(tr) Robert Harding Syndication/Homes & Ideas/Bill Reavell, (br) Abode Interiors, 22(tr) Robert Harding Syndication/Homes & Gardens/Trevor Richards, (cl) Robert Harding Syndication/Homes & Ideas/Andrew Cameron, (br) Eaglemoss/Graham Rae, 23(t) Ducal, (b) Robert Harding Syndication/IPC/Homes & Gardens, 24(cr) Dorma, 24-25 Worldwide Syndication, 26(tr) Next Interior, (cl) Worldwide Syndication, (br) Ducal, 27(tr) Biggie Best, (br) IKEA, 28(tr) The Holding Company, (bl) Dorma, (br) Robert Harding Syndication/Homes & Gardens/Paul Ryan, 29(t) Worldwide Syndication, (br) Ocean Home Shopping, 30-31(tc) Elizabeth Whiting & Associates/Jean-Paul Bonhommet, 30(br) Dulux, 32(tr) IKEA, (cl) Robert Harding Syndication/Homes & Gardens/Pia Tryde, (br) Elizabeth Whiting & Associates/Neil Lorimer, 33 Robert Harding Syndication/Ideal Home/Dominic Blackmore, 34(tc) The Interior Archive/Simon Upton, (c) Robert Harding Syndication/Homes & Gardens/Nadia MacKenzie, (bl) Robert Harding Syndication/Homes & Gardens/Jan Baldwin, (br) Robert Harding Syndication/Homes & Gardens/Tom Leighton, 35-37 Elizabeth Whiting & Associates/Rodney Hyett, 38-39(t) Elizabeth Whiting & Associates, 38(bl) Elizabeth Whiting & Associates/Tom Leighton, (br) Elizabeth Whiting & Associates/Rodney Hyett, 39(tr) Elizabeth Whiting & Associates/Spike Powell, (c) Elizabeth Whiting & Associates/Neil Lorimer, (br) Elizabeth Whiting & Associates/Rodney Hyett, 40(tl) Elizabeth Whiting & Associates/Spike Powell, (tr) Elizabeth Whiting & Associates/Tom Leighton, (bl) McCord, (br) Elizabeth Whiting & Associates/Tom Leighton, 41(t) Worldwide Syndication, (b) IKEA, 42(br) McCord, 42-43(tr) IKEA, 44(tc) BHS, (bl) Hico, (br) IKEA, 44-45(tr) Worldwide Syndication, 45(cr) Robert Harding Syndication/Options/James Merrell, 46(tr) BHS, (cl) Worldwide Syndication, (bl) McCord, (br) Ocean Home Shopping, 47(tr) Robert Harding Syndication/Homes & Gardens/Sandra Lane, (b) Robert Harding Syndication/Homes & Gardens/Polly Wreford, 48(t) Margriet, (b) Eaglemoss/Graham Rae, 49(t) Robert Harding Syndication/Homes & Ideas/Dominic

Blackmore, (b) Harlequin Fabrics, 50(t) Robert Harding Syndication/Ideal Home/Graham Rae, (b) Robert Harding Syndication/Homes & Gardens/Trevor Richards, 51(t) Ariadne, Holland, (b) Robert Harding Syndication/Woman & Home/Debi Treloar, 52(t) Robert Harding Syndication/Country Homes & Interiors/Christopher Drake, (b) Robert Harding Syndication/Ideal Home/Lucinda Symons, 53 Robert Harding Syndication/Homes & Gardens/Tom Leighton, 54(tl) Abode Interiors, (bl) Magriet, 54-55(br) Abode Interiors, 55(t) Robert Harding Syndication/Homes & Gardens/Polly Wreford, (br) Elizabeth Whiting & Associates/Spike Powell, 56(tr) Elizabeth Whiting & Associates/Di Lewis, (bl) Elizabeth Whiting & Associates/Andreas von Einsiedel, 57(t) Abode Interiors, (bl) Robert Harding Syndication/Ideal Home/Polly Wreford, (br) Eaglemoss/Lizzie Orme, 58(t) Cy deCosse, (c) Robert Harding Syndication/Homes & Gardens/Debi Treloar, (bl) Cy deCosse, (br) Robert Harding Syndication/Country Homes & Interiors/James Merrell, 59 Robert Harding Syndication/Country Homes & Interiors/Polly Wreford, 60(tr) Dulux, 60(br) Robert Harding Syndication/Country Homes & Interiors/M Crockett, (br) Elizabeth Whiting & Associates/Mark Luscombe-Whyte, 61(tr) Harlequin Fabrics, (br) Hamerville/Home Flair, 62(tr) Ariadne, Holland, (b) Elizabeth Whiting & Associates/Nick Carter, 63(tr) Robert Harding Syndication/Homes & Ideas/Dominic Blackmore, (bl) Elizabeth Whiting & Associates/Spike Powell, 64(tr) Worldwide Syndication, (cl) Dulux, (bl) Crowson Fabrics, 65 Harlequin Fabrics, 66 Next Interior, 67(t,b) Dulux, 68(t) Elizabeth Whiting & Associates/Andreas von Einsiedel, (b) Robert Harding Syndication/Ideal Home/Dominic Blackmore, 69(t) Robert Harding Syndication/Ideal Home/Polly Wreford, (b) Robert Harding Syndication/Homes & Gardens/Trevor Richards, 70(tr) Dulux, (cl) Cy deCosse, (bl) Robert Harding Syndication/Homes & Gardens/Tim Beddow, (br) Robert Harding Syndication/Homes & Ideas/Dominic Blackmore, 71 Robert Harding Syndication/Homes & Gardens/Trevor Richards, 72(tl) Robert Harding Syndication/IPC/Country Homes & Interiors, 72-73(bl) Robert Harding Syndication/Homes & Gardens/Tom Leighton, 73(tr) Robert Harding Syndication/Country Homes & Interiors/Nadia MacKenzie, (br) Robert Harding Syndication/Country Homes & Interiors/Lucinda Symons, 74(tr) Robert Harding Syndication/Homes & Ideas/Polly Wreford, (bl) Next Interior, (br) Robert Harding Syndication/Homes & Gardens/Trevor Richards, 75(tc) Robert Harding Syndication/Homes & Ideas/Polly Wreford, (cr) Robert Harding Syndication/Homes & Gardens/John Ferris, (br) Elizabeth Whiting & Associates/Mark Luscombe-Whyte, 76(tr) Abode Interiors, (cl) Robert Harding Syndication/IPC/Homes & Gardens, (bl) Robert Harding Syndication/Homes & Gardens/Debbie Patterson, (bc) Robert Harding Syndication/Homes & Gardens/Henry Bourne, 77 Elizabeth Whiting & Associates/Dennis Stone, 78(tr) Ocean Home Shopping, (b) Do It All, 79(t) Hamerville/Home Flair, (b) Robert Harding Syndication/Ideal Home/Dominic Blackmore, 80(tl) Harlequin Fabrics, (tr) Rufflette, (br) Romo Ltd, 81(tr)

Fine Decor, (b) Abode Interiors, 82(tr) Robert Harding Syndication/Ideal Home/Lucinda Symons, (bl) Harlequin Fabrics, (br) Elizabeth Whiting & Associates/Di Lewis, 83(t) Elizabeth Whiting & Associates/Mark Nicholson, (cr) The Photographers Library, (br) The Image Bank, 84(tr) The Image Bank, (cl) Elizabeth Whiting & Associates/Tim Street-Porter, (br) The Image Bank, 85(tl) Elizabeth Whiting & Associates/Mark Nicholson, (bl) The Image Bank, (br) Elizabeth Whiting & Associates/Rodney Hyett, 86(tc) The Image Bank, (cl) Abode Interiors, (br) Elizabeth Whiting & Associates/Neil Lorimer, 87(tr) Elizabeth Whiting & Associates/Andreas von Einsiedel, (cr,bc) The Image Bank, 88(tr) Elizabeth Whiting & Associates/Ian Parry, (cr,br) The Image Bank, (bl) Elizabeth Whiting & Associates/Mark Nicholson, 89 Robert Harding Syndication/Country Homes & Interiors, 90(tl) Eaglemoss/Graham Rae, (tr) Elizabeth Whiting & Associates/Spike Powell, (bl) Robert Harding Syndication/Homes & Gardens/Jan Baldwin, 91(tl) Eaglemoss/Graham Rae, (tr) Hamerville/Home Flair, (bl) Elizabeth Whiting & Associates/Brian Harrison, 92(tr) B&Q, (cl) Eaglemoss/Graham Rae, (b) Elizabeth Whiting & Associates/Mark Luscombe-Whyte, 93(tr,bl) Abode Interiors, (br) Eaglemoss/Graham Rae, 94(tr) Elizabeth Whiting & Associates/Tom Leighton, (cl) Robert Harding Syndication/Homes & Gardens/Jan Baldwin, (bl) Robert Harding Syndication/Ideal Home/Trevor Richards, (br) Elizabeth Whiting & Associates/Di Lewis, 95 Elizabeth Whiting & Associates/Simon Upton, 96(tc) Robert Harding Syndication/Options/Nick Pope, (cl) Elizabeth Whiting & Associates/Jean-Paul Bonhommet, (br) Robert Harding Syndication/Homes & Gardens/Christopher Drake, 97 Robert Harding Syndication/Options/James Merrell, 98 (tr) Elizabeth Whiting & Associates/Simon Upton, (cl) Abode Interiors, (br) Elizabeth Whiting & Associates/Rodney Hyett, 99(bl,br) Marie Claire Maison/Marie Pierre Morel/Gael Reyre, 100(tr) Robert Harding Syndication/Homes & Gardens/Christopher Drake, (cl) Robert Harding Syndication/Ideal Home/Nadia MacKenzie, (bc) Abode Interiors, 101-103 Eaglemoss/Lizzie Orme, 104(tl) Eaglemoss/Steve Tanner, (cr) Arcaid/Jeremy Cockayne, (b) Eaglemoss/Graham Rae, 105-108 Eaglemoss/Lizzie Orme, 108(tr) Robert Harding Syndication/Country Homes and Interiors, 109-110 Eaglemoss/Steven Pam, 111(t) Eaglemoss/Steve Pam, (br) Elizabeth Whiting & Associates, 112 Eaglemoss/Steve Pam, 113 Eaglemoss/Graham Rae, 114 Eaglemoss/Lizzie Orme 115(t) Robert Harding Syndication/Country Homes & Interiors, (b) Eaglemoss/Lizzie Orme, 116(t) Eaglemoss/Lizzie Orme, (c) Robert Harding Syndication/IPC/Country Homes & Interiors, (b) Robert Harding Syndication/IPC/Homes & Ideas, 117-120 Eaglemoss/Graham Rae, 121-123 Eaglemoss/Lizzie Orme, 124(t) Cy deCosse, (cl) Robert Harding Syndication/Homes & Gardens/Les Meeham, (bc) Robert Harding Syndication/Homes & Ideas/Dominic Blackmore, (br) Hamerville/Home Flair, 125-126 Eaglemoss/Graham Rae.